I0474177

The Art of the Consultative Sales Process

Insurance Sales Made Easy

By Paul Donovan

Featuring the new PARC System of Discovery

Selling an intangible product like insurance, offers many unique challenges to the sales person. Many of the concepts I've written about can transfer easily into other service oriented sales. However, this book addresses the main concerns specific to the insurance profession. That's right, this book is for those that want to stop the quoting game and start the winning process. Applying these principals will help you become the consultative insurance professional that agents and brokers aspire to be and that businesses want to work with. The only requirements are an extremely high ethical standard, a willingness to learn and lots of hard work.

Paul Donovan

DEDICATION

To Jan, Kevin & Connor - The Donovan Family

Table of Contents

Part 3

Essentials of the Insurance Professional

Preface

- If you were provided a proven method for increasing your sales results, how valuable would that be?

I wish someone had asked me that question when I had first started my sales career. It would have saved me so much wasted energy, time, frustration and money. I've been a career commissioned insurance sales professional for the past two and a half decades. Earning only what I could kill/close, with no guarantee of income. You can imagine my amusement with the word "budget." Having walked the proverbial mile in the moccasins, I have extreme empathy for my fellow sales professionals. The people we most respect in life are the ones that have been where we are and have gone through the same experiences and can empathize. Like most people with any length of time in sales, I've been ranked everywhere from dead last in production to number one. Rest assured, being at the bottom of the pack is not as much fun as being at the top. The pressures from the lack of production do not solely affect ones finances. It can greatly impact your emotions, self-confidence, attitudes, behaviors, and even your character if you let it. If I could go back in time, this is the book I would have handed myself at the very beginning of my journey. Permit me to share with you my experiences.

Throughout my life I have been insanely curious, asking questions and seeking answers, much to the chagrin of my teachers. Even as a young teen, I vividly remember having some pretty deep nagging questions. Not just questions about what I was going to be when I grew up, I mean deep philosophical questions like:

- What's the meaning of life and does my life have a purpose?
- What's the secret to success?
- How do I know this isn't all just a big dream?
- Why can't the Red Sox win the World Series (even then, I knew there were certain mysteries only God could answer)?

Curiosity mixed with an extremely competitive spirit fueled my search for the ultimate sales system. There had to be a system that was based on truth, was consultative in nature and geared to my career choice. My journey led me to attend numerous sales training seminars, read lots of books and study many of the more popular sales systems. The saying, *"A picture is worth a thousand words,"* is a quick reminder how a beautiful canvas or photograph can convey a complex idea and affect our senses with a single image. If a picture is worth a thousand words, then an experience is worth a thousand pictures. My education comes from experience, study and observation. Sometimes you have to experience things first hand in order to truly learn. Other times, just seeing the results or reading a story is enough for us to emulate or avoid a behavior. For instance, one doesn't have to become a drug addict to understand the consequences and hurt that that would have on mind and body.

The Boy Scout motto is, "Be prepared." Basketball coach, Bobby Knight, said, *"The will to win is not nearly as important as the will to prepare to win."* In sales you don't have just one chance to win, but you don't have unlimited opportunities either. The business of sales is "selling as much as you can, given the time permitted." In today's competitive sales culture, where time is of the essence, most can't afford the luxury of "blowing," too many opportunities while attending the school of hard knocks.

If you're like me, you've probably had managers that were great when it came to accountability but poor when it came to coaching and mentoring. Having spent time in the trenches I'm decidedly seasoned enough to share some of the answers I've found along my journey. Friends have jokingly commented about my seasoned career, stating, "It's taken him years to get his head together and now his body is falling apart." This book is practical and will help you:

> Avoid the most common sales mistakes that are made
> Develop a consultative approach
> Increase your success ratio at a faster pace
> Get rid of some head trash & have more fun

A consultative style means a lot less pressure than many traditional methods. Professional salesmanship is a process that takes discipline, and hard work. In my own zeal and thirst for knowledge, I well remember that information overload sometimes feels like taking a drink from a fire hydrant. In logic we learned about **Ockham's razor,** expressed in **Latin** as the *lex parsimoniae*, translating to the law of parsimony or succinctness. In today's lingo, "keep it simple." If it's too complicated or hard to remember, you'll never use it. I also wanted to introduce numerous true accounts from over twenty five years of selling insurance. This lends to credibility and not just theory. Naturally, for reasons of privacy and confidentiality, I've carefully changed a few details, while keeping the integrity of the story. Some sales books formulate hypothetical conversation scenarios between prospects and sales people. I've chosen to offer practical principles relayed through true stories learned in the trenches. You may determine, as I did, that having a great supply of questions at your disposal is far more valuable than rehearsing a scene that may or may not come to pass.

We all learn at a young age that perfection is a process that eludes us all. Therefore, the goal has always been to obtain consistent incremental improvement that draws us nearer to the mark. I'm confident that you will be able to mine a few golden nuggets from the principals inside. The fact that you are reading this means you are committed to self improvement. Whether you're a seasoned professional that just needs a boost, or a rookie looking for some guidance, these ideas work and will help you succeed.

This book is divided into three main sections.

I.   The First section deals with an easy to recall system for the foundations of consultative sales. It also speaks to our attitudes, behaviors and beliefs that are critical to establishing and maintaining the right outlook for success.

II. The Second section deals with the PARC System of discovery. It provides numerous examples of questions specific to a consultative sales practice and process.

III. The Third section contains a brief toolbox of skill sets that sales professionals must carry with them. Sales professionals implement techniques, processes and habits that can be taught, learned and replicated. Hundreds of sales books and courses on sales and the art of selling have been written about these skills and techniques (including this one).

Please Note:

- Throughout the book I preface most questions with a declaration bullet, watch for them, ponder and answer honestly.

"Advice is what we ask for when we already know the answer but wish we didn't."
Erica Jong

Introduction to Lessons Learned

An Early Start

I'm the typical American male, the last of the "Baby Boomers" generation. Raised in a suburb south of Boston called Brockton, Massachusetts. A great blue-collar town known as the City of Champions; affiliated with Rocky Marciano (the only undefeated heavyweight boxing champion in the world) and Marvelous Marvin Hagler (the middle weight boxing champ throughout the 1980's).

Having a mom as a teacher in Plymouth, I fully understood the term "Puritan Work Ethic." I have been working, earning, and saving money since I was kid. At eleven years old I delivered the morning newspapers from my bicycle at 5:00AM. In the winter or during heavy rain, I rode up hill both ways in the sleet and snow (just in case my children ever read this). My route allowed me barely enough time to scramble home, change my clothes and run to catch the bus. After school and homework I completed my chores. Every Friday afternoon I would retrace my route stopping by each house for "collections" of the weekly papers and tips. Christmas time was a paperboy's lottery. In addition to homemade treats, one could make as much as three month's wages (about $150). Throughout my school days, I held various jobs working at the fish docks, in restaurants, landscaping, roofing and ditch digging. Continuously learning, gaining experience, I still lacked satisfaction. While my discontent grew, I maintained my Christian values and commitment to excellence.

"Whatever you do, work at it with all your heart, as working for the Lord, not for human masters, 24 since you know that you will receive an inheritance from the Lord as a reward. It is the Lord Christ you are serving." Colossians 3:23 NIV

Choices

It's not only *what* a person does that is a "calling," but *how* you do what you do, that matters. Fulfilling your "call," is about exceeding

expectations and performing with excellence in whatever you are doing.
Great philosophy, yup, but I still wondered how did one choose a fulfilling career? I admired those few souls that knew exactly what they wanted to be when they grew up. Maybe I didn't dream big enough to find this elusive destiny but one thing was for sure, my hunt and peck method sure was exhausting. After graduating high school my father strongly suggested I had only two choices, either college or the military. It was a hard decision because I truly love and wanted to serve my country. After some soul searching, I thought, throughout my lifetime every authority figure and successful person I had ever heard had preached, "Gaining an education was the ticket to a better life." I therefore chose to attend college with hopes of obtaining that ticket. Like most late teens away from home for the first time, I was no longer shackled to the restraints of parents. I was finally free to make my own decisions, to discover, be independent, and be my own boss! That is… until my parents put conditions upon the tuition checks I needed (coupled with student loans). **Lesson learned**: freedom is usually tethered to a bank account.

Life Changer

Thankfully, college had a monumental life changing affect on me and I still feel its impact to this day. For it was in college that I met the most incredible person in the world. She had pierced my very soul and still remains the love of my life, my bride, best friend, confidant and partner. After graduation we married. Gaining an education gave me a degree but I still felt aimless, lacking direction toward a career path to pursue (or so I thought). **Lesson learned**: finding a spouse that is passionately committed to you, unconditionally supportive of your efforts and is contagiously encouraging, makes your life 99.9% easier! Having officially entered "bread winner," status, I seriously required a job. The great Victorian England essayist Thomas Carlyle said, "*A man without a purpose is like a ship without a rudder.*" As a Christian, I believe that God has a purpose for each of our lives. It was time to cease flapping my sails in the wind, gain some direction and fulfill my calling. Stepping out in faith truly is a four letter word spelled RISK.

The Rookie

Insurance has been in my blood since I was a kid. You see, my dad had been in the insurance industry all of his life. He held a variety of insurance positions in claims, sales and underwriting. I vividly remember him telling me, "Son, there's no cap on your salary when you are in sales, you're paid what you are worth." That made sense. However, I've always wanted to be fair with myself and others. After all, a clean conscience is the softest pillow. I asked myself, "Do there have to be winners and losers in sales?" The answer is, "No!" Sales are morally neutral and can be a win for the client, a win for the company and a win for the salesperson. If I were going to pursue a sales career, I would be different. I would avoid the salesman stigma as the fast talking trickster of the carnival midway. Known for:

- ✓ Making exaggerated claims and promises.
- ✓ Not taking "No!" for an answer.
- ✓ Using high pressure closing techniques.

Not wanting to ride the family shirt tails, I independently found an advertisement for an insurance sales position and decided to pursue the opportunity. After all, I liked people and enjoyed the thought of helping others. With preparation, confidence and prayer, I would land my first *real* white collar job with Liberty Mutual Ins. Co. in New City, N.Y. Passing all the state exams, I started in the mid 1980's as a commissioned property and casualty (P&C) agent producer. To say I was green was an understatement. What I lacked in sales skills I made up for with energy and enthusiasm. It was definitely a learning experience and the New York City metro area was a great place to, "cut ones teeth." Unfortunately, the main content of my education consisted of product knowledge rather than actual sales training. I would follow the same path that so many people before me had set out on. A management led pathway of high activity that produced initial high "apptivity." Apptivity is the numbers game of placing large amounts of applications. Faithfully I submitted everything and anything with hopes that a majority of it would pass underwriting and stick. The pressures of new business production drove me to work long hours. Nevertheless, after only three years, I was leading my entire office in new business production month over month. My efforts were paying off monetarily and I was being recognized as a leader. Now there's an old quote that says, *"I thought I wanted a career, turns out I really just wanted paychecks."* I originally landed the position as a method to make money in a white collar profession. **Lesson learned**: A taste of success instills confidence. This confidence became the launching pad for my decision to make a career in insurance sales.

Learning Curve

Perhaps in retrospect, some of my success was due to my feverish activity level and some competitive pricing rather than my savvy sales skills. Then, as so often happens in every sales person's career, I hit a "dry-spell." My approach remained the same but my results were off. I took logical steps and went from a self imposed fifty hour work week to a sixty five hour work week. Logically thinking that the more time I put into it, my results would improve. It worked for a while, but one can only stay on that treadmill for so long before exhaustion sets in and your psyche is impacted. Survival instincts kicked in and quickly I realized something had to change. I recalled an incident from my childhood days. I remember asking a teacher a simple clarification over the spelling of a word. The reply I received was, "Go look it up in the dictionary." I remember thinking to myself at the time, "Well if I knew how to spell it in the first place I could and would look it up!" **Lesson learned**: if you're inquisitive and want great answers, be prepared for hard work and research. I already knew how to work hard, now I needed to work smart. I knew the professional surpasses the amateur based on their commitments. Therefore, I would become a student of sales, investing time and money in pursuit of professionalism.

The formula and pattern for the development of a sale

Most of the more popular sales training curriculum provided great foundations. I would typically find a pearl inside each of them that I could benefit from. However, there was a twist of irony. It seemed the more books and systems I read and explored, the more contradictions I came across. Why did some of the best sales experts give seemingly conflicting advice? Why did some techniques work in some sales scenarios and not in others? The mystery grew and I was about to make a breakthrough. As my Irish luck would have it, I came across a great book that helped me decipher why some sales experts differed so greatly. In his monumental best-selling book, SPIN Selling, Neil Rackman reviewed the traditional sales cycle.

1. **Opening the call** – building rapport
2. **Investigating the needs** – open & closed ended questioning
3. **Giving benefits** – uncover needs, then show how features can benefit the prospect
4. **Objection Handling** – overcoming objections (clarifying, rewording etc.)
5. **Closing Techniques** – commonly taught techniques

His investigation showed these methods worked for smaller simple sales but **not** necessarily for larger sales. He validated his research through the study of over 35,000 sales calls. He confirmed that *large sales share similar characteristics.* They typically have:

1. Longer sales cycle.
2. Longer cycle translates into multiple customer contacts.
3. A multi-call selling cycle has a different psychology. A good product pitch can have a temporary effect on a customer (they are enthusiastic, they like you etc.) but when they have to go back and sell it to their boss and their bosses boss on a major purchase, the memory tends to fade and translation becomes muddled.
4. Larger sales include multiple decision makers.
5. The larger the decision the more cautious the prospect becomes.

Wow, what worked in one size of sale didn't necessarily work in another. In the insurance field, we commonly find ourselves selling to BOTH large (relationship driven) and small (transaction driven) accounts. What a revelation, one size doesn't fit all! With this knowledge I could decide what types of accounts to target, how to approach them and what steps would best win. A humorous side note: Through a quirk of fate, years later I would develop and teach this information to others.

Fresh Start

Back to the career. My wife had casually mentioned that eventually she would like to move back to Florida to be nearer her parents. We decided that we would take a gamble and on January 1, 1991, we packed our belongings and moved to the sunshine state. We were young, it was an adventure and Florida would be a fresh start. I secured a job with a small independent agency as a producer and started to build a book of business. I was finally beginning to understand Shakespeare. In his play, As you Like It, he said, *"All the world's a stage and we are merely players each one having his exits and his entrances. His acts being seven ages, infant, schoolboy, lover, soldier middle age then reverting back to old age and childhood."* Experience is change and experience is seasoning. Over the next decade I would make partner, leave, spend another decade with two different national firms, traverse a merger and finally start my own firm.

Throughout all the success, I still felt there was something missing; there was a growing restlessness inside me. I would wrestle with concepts such as, adding value to the client (what did that meant and how is it done?). Margins were shrinking and maintaining production goals were becoming more difficult. I was tired of using obsolete prospecting methods and I desperately needed something new. I wanted a resource that answered all of my questions under one roof. I had the basic sales skills of, prospecting, qualifying, resolving needs, talking with the decision maker, confronting the replacement of the incumbent and closing the sale. What I noticed was that there were very little specific resources on consultative sales in my industry of insurance sales. I began to piece together my own resources based on the techniques, behaviors and experiences I had that were successful. The results, is this book.

"There's no sense giving someone a rose to smell once you've chopped off their nose."
Ravi Zacharias

PART I
ATTITUDES BEHAVIORS AND BELIEFS

Chapter 1

Sales 101?

When we think of the word *"sales"* or *"selling"*, what comes to mind? Most would agree, we think of sales in terms of transferring a product or service to someone in return for money and selling as the act of influencing or persuading someone to buy. These definitions explain what sales and selling is, but not how sales are accomplished. If you have ever had a job, a date, or a dog you know about persuasion. The power to influence others is tough, but have you ever thought about why people buy? Do you think it was for *your* reasons or for *their* reasons? Sales methods can be risky and confusing. I once jokingly stated that sales systems are like cults, there's an element of truth in each of them. While that's probably overstating, I'm convinced that most sales books and sales systems offer something valuable in the form of a tool, tip or technique, that will help improve your results. After years of studying and applying sales skills, I discovered and had an amazing revelation (my kingdom for a drum roll font). There is no magic bullet and no one specific sales methodology or system that fits every type of sale (product or service), selling style or sales cycle. Successful selling is a combination of skills and attitudes that the sales professional is continuously refining. If there is one universal message consistent among all types of sales, it boils down to one word, "Trust." Successful selling is ultimately based in trust.

Quick History of American Trust

America was founded Judeo Christian principles or what is commonly referred to as the Christian worldview. A world view is a philosophy of life that each of us has. It's the framework of ideas, attitudes and beliefs that guide a person's life. In short, a person's core convictions determine their worldview. Our founding fathers saw man as an individual creation of God, special in his own right, worthy and valued as an individual. By breaking our ties with mother England, we evoked the "Classless Society."

No longer would authority be granted through inherited birthright. No longer would we put our trust in a royal hierarchy. Distinctions of wealth, education, and social network would be determined by individual achievement which would assure each person, freedom, liberty and justice. This was the basis of the Declaration of Independence, our Constitution and the Bill of Rights. This new opportunity created wave after wave of migration for those that wanted to *trust* in a better way of life. Generally, we Americans share a few common beliefs that transcend our multi-ethnic lines. We believe in:

- ✓ The American Dream = the Pursuit of Happiness.
- ✓ American Exceptionalism.

By exceptionalism I mean, we have a history of trust in healthy individualism. We trust our government to not interfere with the legal pursuit of our choice. As a competitive culture we believe our products, processes and people set the standard for the world to meet. As long as there is a level playing field we each have the freedom to succeed or fail based on the right amount of determination, persistence, ingenuity and enthusiasm. In essence, exceptionalism means, "freedom."

"If you have a dream, give it a chance to happen."
Richard de Vos

Why Trust

On my quest for answers, I found a clue to what brings meaning to life. Ponder to think about it.

- "What is it that is valued most by every human being?

Regardless of culture, economic circumstances, where you are from, what you look like or who your family is. Irrespective of the time in history that mankind finds himself in, the answer is always the same. The most important and valuable thing in life is our *relationships*. You never hear people on their deathbed saying, "I wish I had spent more time at the office!" No, it's our associations with others that reigns supreme. The relationships we establish with God, family, friends, colleagues, community, clients, vendors and even our pets, that's what's important.

What gives these relationships so much value is the level of trust we come to expect from them. Trust is a firm reliance on the integrity, ability or character of a person. Trustworthy people gain our assurance that they will not take advantage of us and that they have our best interests at heart. The depth of relationships comes when each partner asks themselves the crucial questions:

1. Can I trust you?
2. Are you committed?
3. How much time will you invest?
4. Do you care about me?

Who do we trust? In our society we typically trust policemen, firemen, and clergy. These men and women project safety and protection with which we can place our care. Those attributes develop confidence and confidence equals security. Relationship selling helps establish and grow trust. When a prospect knows you have their best interest at heart first (trust) there is typically a good fit.

Change is necessary for growth and growth is the lifeblood of relationships and business. My friend Bill says, "In business you have three choices, you grow, you sell or you die." If you want to become better in business, become better at sustaining relationships. To become better at relationships you need to be trusted, committed and have a high level of care for others. Only then will you grow, thrive and truly live.

"To be trusted is a greater compliment than to be loved."
George MacDonald

There is only one boss: The CUSTOMER. And he can fire everybody in the company, from the chairman on down, simply by spending his money somewhere else. Sam Walton (founder of Walmart)

Chapter 2
The easiest way to remember?

With the advantages of WebMD and other medical websites, access to information is more plentiful than ever before. Am I the only one to have self diagnosed myself with a problem just by doing research concerning the symptoms? Although never *"officially"* diagnosed, looking back, I think I may have had Attention Deficit Hyperactivity Disorder (A.D.H.D.) as a child. Unfortunately my father made his own home made Ritalin and he called it a "belt." I joke now, but I truly did have trouble concentrating on one thing for any period of time. I was constantly thinking two steps ahead before confirming previous ones. Innocently I would sometimes frustrate myself and others. I needed help and I found it within the study of mnemonics. Mnemonics is any learning device that aids in memory. The word is derived from the ancient Greek word Mnemosyne (the Greek goddess of memory). Since we were children, teachers have used acronyms, songs and poems to help us remember things. It's no different in sales. With so many things to remember, it's easy to get confused. Acronyms are an easy way to focus our attention and package complex ideas into in an easy to remember word. The first acronym I remember learning was KISS. It stood for Keep It Simple Stupid. It's simple, effective and easy to remember. Spend enough time in any sales organization and you will eventually hear words like: SALE, SELL, SPIN, AIDA, LAIR, FAB, LACE, FAVOR, TRUST and RISK.

S - serving

A - asking

L - istening

E - excelling

S - situation

P - problem

I - implication

N - need (payoff)

S - show

E - explain

L - lead to buy

L - let them talk

A - attention

I - interest

D - desire

A - action

L - listen
A - acknowledge
I - identify objection
R - reverse it

L - Listen
A - Accept
C - commit
E - explicit action

T - Transparency
R - Relationship
U - United
S - Secure
T - Team,

F - features
A - attributes or advantages
B - benefits

F - fact or feature
A - associated function / purpose
V - validate evidence/ experience
O - obvious advantage or benefit
R - ratify or secure agreement

R - Relationship
I - Integrity
S - Serve
K - Kindness

For an interesting guide to government abbreviations and acronyms visit, **www.govspeak.com**.

As a society we are fully immersed in the age of information. Technology has granted us unparalleled access to facts and figures at the speed of our fingertips. With this media bombardment I'm convinced we have also lost a portion of our capacity to concentrate. Don't get me wrong, I love my gadgets too, but it's a wonder we can remember anything at all. Am I the only one with passworditus? Thankfully, the most basic tool for systematically organizing thoughts lies within the acronym.

"I always have trouble remembering three things: faces, names, and - I can't remember what the third thing is".
Fred Allen

Chapter 3

PALACES

When you think of a palace you might think of The Biltmore Estate, Versailles, The Forbidden City or Neuschwanstein Castel. All of them, great homes built from great wealth. But true wealth has nothing to do with the possessions or net worth that one has. True wealth is characterized by the quality of your relationships, pursuing your passions and living life with a purpose.

P = **Passion**
A = **Attitude**
L = **Listening**
A = **Aim**
C = **Character**
E = **Endurance**
S = **Setbacks**

PALACES is an acronym for the seven attributes that sales professionals must learn to improve and develop to obtain success.

Passion

When Vince Lombardi took over as coach for the Green Bay Packers he was not handed a winning team. In 1958 the Packers were at the bottom of the division, they lost ten out of 12 games, tied one and won one. When he addressed the players at spring training camp in June of 1959 Lombardi was faced with a dispirited football team. According to an article in Guidepost magazine, Lombardi said, "Gentlemen, we are going to have a great football team. We are going to win games. Get that!" "Now, how are we going to accomplish that?" He continued, "You are going to learn to block, run, and tackle. You are going to outplay all the teams that come up against you. Get that!" Then he said, "You are going to have confidence in me and enthusiasm for my system. Hereafter, I want you to think of only three things: your home, your religion and the Green Bay Packers, in that order! Let enthusiasm take hold of you beginning now!"

He told them, "If you aren't fired with enthusiasm, you will be fired, with enthusiasm!" Virtually the same players as the year before went on to win seven games that year, the division title the next year and the world championship in the third year. Their renewed passion for the game produced astounding results.

- How would a renewed enthusiasm for what you do enhance the outcome?
- How would your mood, actions and performance be altered if you knew that being unenthusiastic would get you fired?

Retired CEO Jack Welch (Winning) had a formula he used when hiring new employees, he called it the: 4 Es + 1 P. He said, "Passion is the juice of life." And employees need to show:

E – Positive Enthusiasm
E – Energize others around you
E – Edge – has the courage to make yes or no (tough) decisions
E – Execution or the ability to get the job done because winning is about results
P - Passion is loving what you do and having enthusiasm

Have you ever met someone that has found their calling in life and is passionate about it? You can see it in their eyes, feel it in the pump of their handshake and hear it in their voice. You know they love what they do.

I have a friend and mentor in life that I remember meeting for the first time in his office. He's a world famous eye surgeon and absolutely loves what he does. As I entered his clinic he was obviously extremely busy, but found time to want to meet with me in between patients. He ushered me into a patient waiting room and to my surprise, introduced me to his latest patient and her husband. His enthusiasm over how he fixed her vision from near blindness to now seeing better than 20/20 was contagious. He had the nurse take a picture with an instant camera and insisted that I be in the picture with him and the patient's family. He wanted everyone to know how happy he was for the blessing of correcting someone's sight, and he captured it for the patient with a keepsake memory. It was one of the rare occasions I witnessed someone truly enthusiastic for having the opportunity to work and loving what they do. My friend has a rare combination of contagious enthusiasm mixed with humility of spirit. He is also one of the most generous men I know. Why is that kind of passion so rare? I think it's because too many people are just going through the motions in their employment and they don't love what they do. When you don't love what you do it's even harder to love your clients and customers. This will directly affect your productivity, income and success. Money is a great motivator but it will not satisfy you if you don't love what you do. It may provide for your lifestyle, but it will leave a vacuum in your inner being.

If you are contemplating entering sales or are already in sales, it's time you ask yourself some important questions.

1. Why are you in sales in the first place? Some may respond they are in it for the freedom it provides and/or the money. The ultimate question that needs to be answered is, what is it you LOVE to do? Then go do it.

2. If you didn't have to worry about finances and you could do anything that you really wanted to do, what would you be doing? The answer to that question will determine the amount of true passion and your attitude that you exhibit on a daily basis. I asked the person that cuts my hair that very question. She said, "Paul, I am doing what I love, I'd be cutting hair!" Isn't that awesome? Wouldn't you rather have your hair cut by someone that loves what they do? The next time you see a friend that looks like a blind man with hiccups cut their hair, ask them to ask their hair stylist/barber the same question.

3. If you love what you do but don't like your current job, it may be time to ask why? Is it the people, product, or services you're selling (perhaps it's your attitude that needs to change)? Life is

too short, either you change yourself or change your environment (perhaps you change both).

4. If you were the owner of the organization, how would you rate your performance and effort? Sometimes the reason sales people are unhappy with their current position is because they haven't performed up to expectations and that has snowballed into pressure. If that's the case, the first thing to change is your attitude.

Ultimately, no one can control you but you. It comes from knowing your convictions and core beliefs. What you think about, either positive or negative, will determine how you behave.

"As you begin changing your thinking, start immediately to change your behavior. Begin to act the part of the person you would like to become. Take action on your behavior. Too many people want to feel, then take action. This never works."
John Maxwell

"Nothing can stop the man with the right mental attitude from achieving his goal; nothing on earth can help the man with the wrong mental attitude."
Thomas Jefferson

Attitude

Don't you wish you were best friends with C. W. Longenecker? Who is he you ask? The great C. W. Longenecker is not a household name but he should be. He wrote a masterpiece poem on attitude.

> If you *think* you are beaten, you are,
> If you *think* you dare not, you don't,
> If you like to win, but you *think* you can't,
> It is almost certain you won't
>
> If you *think* you'll lose you're lost,
> For out in the world we find,
> Success begins with a fellow's will,
> It's all in a *state of mind.*
>
> If you *think* you're outclassed, you are,
> You've got to *think* high to rise,
> You've got to be *sure of yourself* before
> You can ever win the prize.
>
> Life's battles don't always go,
> To the strongest or faster man,
> But sooner or later the man who wins
> Is the man WHO THINKS HE CAN!

The way you think affects your attitudes and actions either positively or negatively. Consider the people you know and associate with regularly. Are they mostly positive in their outlooks or do they put a negative spin on everything? Consider this.

- If you haven't met your quota or sales objectives, could it be that negative thinking and attitude has played a role in that?
- Are your thoughts mostly positive or negative?
- Do you expect to win more than you expect to lose, or the other way around?

A positive attitude precedes positive actions. What do you see below?

HEISNOWHERE

Do you see <u>He Is No Where</u> (negative) or do you see <u>He Is Now Here</u> (positive)? It all depends on how you look at it. Fix your mindset and rest assured.

Opportunity is NOWHERE (Now Here)

Changes in actions come from changes in thinking, or "how you see it." You can control and change what you put into your mind. Both the engine in your car and the engine of your body need the proper fuel to make it move. Your body needs healthy nutrition to produce healthy living and so does your mind.

- How much and what type of brain fuel are you feeding your mind?
- Do you watch too much trash television, sitcoms, reality TV, news, newspapers?

I am not advocating media abstinence; rather, I'm supporting a new mind fuel injection service.

- What was the last positive book you read?
- What inspires you daily to be your best?
- What proactive steps are you taking to renew your mindset?

Expecting to achieve your goals for the day will greatly increase your chances of success. After all, if you can only manage what you can control, then, the only thing you have absolute control over is your attitude. Other people don't determine my happiness and they shouldn't determine yours. Ultimately we are responsible for how we feel. With the exception of some medically diagnosed chemical deficiencies, most people have the ability or the "will" to determine their attitudes throughout the day. *"As a man thinks in his heart so is he."* (Proverbs 23:7 The Amplified Bible).

The pessimist thinks that someone left a pile of horse manure in the driveway, the optimist is the one looking around for the pony. Here's a quiz. Ask yourself the following questions.

- How's your confidence level? Why?
- What would you do if you knew you couldn't fail?
- Have you taken a risk and tried your best?
- What type of person do you want to be known for?
- Are you the type of person people gravitate towards?

Chuck Swindol writes <u>Attitude is Everything</u>.

"The longer I live, the more I realize the impact of attitude on life. Attitude, to me, is more important that facts. It's more important than the past, than education, than money, than circumstances, than failures, than successes, than what other people think or say or do. It is more important than appearance, giftedness or skill. It will make or break a company, a church, a home. The remarkable thing is we have a choice everyday regarding the attitude we will embrace for that day. We cannot change our past, we cannot change the fact that people will act in a certain way. We cannot change the inevitable. The only thing we can do is play on the one string we have, and that is our attitude. I am convinced that life is 10% what happens to me and 90% how I react to it. And so it is with you as it is with me, we are all in charge of our attitudes."

Life is short and we are on this planet for about seventy to eighty years, give or take. Believing that we are all made in the image of God allows for a healthy self-image. This creates an attitude of gratitude and humility within. One of the slogans on my desk reads, *"In a single day, Samson slew a thousand Philistines with the jawbone of an ass. And every day, thousands of sales are killed with the same weapon!"* Keep life in perspective.

- Are you appreciative for what you've been given?
- Are you thankful for your health, where you live, what you have, who you have relationships with, what you can do?

- Do you realize that there is ALWAYS someone worse off than me and you?

The great Christian thinker G. K. Chesterton tells the story of children waking up on Christmas morning and being surprised and thankful for the socks on the mantle being stuffed with gifts and presents of all types. He goes on to say, if children can be thankful to St. Nicholas for the toys in their socks on Christmas morning, then why can't we be thankful for the two feet God fills in our own socks each day. Truly, it is hard to be depressed when you are grateful. Try this exercise. Make a Gratitude List! Some of the things on my list include my gorgeous smart, industrious wife, my awesome children, family, friends, health, career, colleagues, my dog, great books and living in Florida.

- Who and what is on your list?

Attitude will determine your altitude isn't just a catchy little phrase for motivational posters. Your attitude is also a direct reflection of how you are perceived.

- Have you ever noticed that most successful people hang around with other successful people?
- Do you think that's coincidence?

Very early in my career I remember thinking inappropriate thoughts about my competitors. I thought that the only reason for their success is that I couldn't seem to break into the "good ol boys club" that they were in? These negative thoughts and attitudes of jealousy aren't healthy nor are they going to get you where you want to go. I had the ability to do something about it and I changed my attitude. A positive attitude can be and must be nurtured. Start your day with a positive outlook and carry it with you by being grateful for what you do have, not for what you don't. Only you can choose your attitude.

"Remember, whatever game you play, ninety percent of success is from the shoulders up." Milfred J. "Deacon" Palmer (Arnold Palmer's father)

Listening

Is there any skill in all of the human experience that is so poorly practiced as the art of listening? Is there any skill in all of the human experience that is so poorly practiced as the art of listening? I was just checking on you. *P.S. - This is the only chapter I hope my wife reads with compassion on me.*

Chuck Swindoll tells the story about a consultant in Texas who travels to Germany. The German is explaining to the Texan how large his estate is. He said, "My estate travels as far as that mountain range way off in the distance to the east, then to the large valley to the west. It then goes along hundreds of kilometers towards the river to the south all the way to where we are here." He then asks, "How big is your ranch in Texas?" The Texan very braggingly explains," Well, I can get in my car before the sun comes up and travel all day long and when the sun goes down, I still won't have reached the end of my property!" The German looks at him and says, "I know exactly what you mean, I used to have a car like that too." You see, we sometimes don't speak the same language and that also contributes to our miscommunication and listening skills. Generally, we are so focused on our own agenda about what we do and how we do it, that we lose focus and don't listen to what the other person is saying.

Listening is a skill that must be developed if you want clear communication. Of all the skills to learn, listening is the hardest skill to master. However, when you listen to people you begin to understand what *Journalism 101* calls the; who, what, where, why and how concerns of the individual. You shift your focus on the priorities of the individual speaking, rather than concentrating on your own agenda.

Contrary to some, in the give and take of conversation, the balance in sales rests heavily on the prospect and not on the salesman. Many are familiar with the 80/20 rule known as the Pareto Principle. The Pareto Principal states that twenty percent of the people will be responsible for eighty percent of the production. It should be no different in a conversation with a prospect. The sales person should speak about twenty percent of the time by asking great questions and confirming information. The prospect should be talking eighty percent of the time; telling their story, answering our questions and dialoguing with us in the qualification process. Unfortunately, far too many prospects have been witness to the "show up and throw up," presentation. That's where the salesperson dumps everything they ever learned about their products and services onto the prospect with hopes of somehow hitting a hot spot of interest. Believe me, it's exhausting.

Leo Buscaglia says that, *"Most conversations are just alternating monologues. The question is, is there any real listening going on?"*

For those of us who are members of a family, the examples are endless. If you are not the member of a family, you may have larger concerns! Now this may be a memory issue rather than a listening issue. But, I can't recall the number of times my wife has asked me to go to the grocery store for a handful of items only to have me come home with something completely different or not in the bag at all. I'm thankful for cell phones, for now, I only have to call her a few times from the store in order to accomplish the objective. If a sales person doesn't listen and understand the needs of the prospect, how will they know if their products and services will truly be a benefit?

James Nathan Miller said, *"There is no such thing as a worthless conversation, provided you know what to listen for. Questions, are the breathe of life for a conversation."* Communication doesn't begin with being understood, but with understanding others.

Dale Carnegie had brilliant observations on how to become a great listener and conversationalist in his famous book, <u>How to Win Friends and Influence People</u>. He noticed that every person has a story and if asked they would be willing to share it. One of the keys to becoming a great listener is to ask questions with the words HOW and WHAT. These are known as open-ended questions whereby you can't answer the question with a simple yes or no response. They require more detailed elaboration. Most people love to talk about themselves, their experiences and their loved ones. Asking "how" type questions and being sincerely interested in their story is a great habit to learn and practice. Try it. The next time you have the opportunity to talk with someone ask them a sincere question about:

- How was their experience, please tell me more about it.
- What's your understanding concerning…?
- What have you found?
- What do you look for?
- In your opinion, how do you think this should work?

Nothing is as flattering as exclusive attention to another person when they are talking. And who knows, you may also learn something very exciting. Prospects want to be understood and to understand them you have to listen intently. There's no doubt, the best therapists, counselors, friends and sales people, are those that listen.

Once when I was on a first call with a prospect I had just sat down with the owner of the company and he said, "OK, tell me your spiel." BAMM, right out of the gate! I was a little taken back by his directness, but I could understand the importance of his time. I took a deep breath and slowly and sincerely said, "I don't have a spiel. I typically can't help someone until I understand what it is they do, how that's going and if there is a good fit or not, for our companies to work together. I did some research on your company, but I would really like to know and understand how you started this organization. What got you started?" He sat there in stunned silence for a moment and said, "you know, I see a bunch of sales guys come through my office all the time and all they do is tell me about how great they or their company are. You are one of the few that has ever wondered to ask, what it is I do and what got this started, thank you." I learned a valuable lesson that day. People will always want to tell you about what's most important in their life if you sincerely ask and want to know.

- Try this: Find a great listener and observe them in a conversation. Pay attention to their eyes, body language, and percentage of speaking they do in a conversation.

The top 10 Keys to Effective Listening

1. Hold your fire - Resist the urge to interrupt. Allow the speaker to finish their thoughts.
2. Maintain eye contact - when you are looking in a person's eyes they know you are paying attention.
3. Affirm with verbal feedback and when appropriate ask clarifying questions.
4. Resist distractions - focus on the person.
5. Listen for the real message - the person speaking may reveal concerns you did not know existed.
6. Listen with respect and validation - make the choice to be interested.
7. Listen without thinking about how you are going to respond.
8. Take notes - ask permission to take them (you will never be denied).
9. Body language - research has shown that more than seventy-five percent of our communication is non-verbal (Lean forward slightly; nod your head that you understand etc.)
10. Put yourself in their shoes - try to empathize with them when they are discussing a situation or circumstance.

Listening skills can be developed, and like any muscle, with exercise and time comes strength and growth. If you want to be heard, first begin by listening to others. The old Rough Rider and President, Teddy Roosevelt said, *"Nobody cares how much you know until they know how much you care."* Did you say something?

A=X+Y+Z "If A equals success, then the formula is A equals X plus Y and Z, with X being work, Y play, and Z keeping your mouth shut."
Albert Einstein

"If a woman speaks and no one is listening, her name is probably mom."

Aim

Why is it important to have aim in life? What a great question. Goal setting is one of the first steps towards achievement and success. We know that our core values ultimately shape the motives for our actions. It has to do with our internal wants and needs and how we can gain pleasure and avoid fear/pain. But why are they important? Because it's a lot harder to reach the next point when you fire before you aim! If you aim at nothing you will hit it every time. John Condry said, *"Happiness, wealth, and success are by-products of goal setting. They cannot be the goal themselves."* Therefore, just wanting to be successful is not a goal. Better planning equals better success and your goals must be written out. Goals can be set in almost every area of our multi-faceted lives.

- ✓ Family Goals
- ✓ Physical/Health Goals
- ✓ Educational Goals
- ✓ Spiritual Goals
- ✓ Career Goals
- ✓ Financial Goals and many more

<u>Where do you begin?</u>

Early in my career I was taught a very simple and well known acronym when setting goals called **S.M.A.R.T.** goals.

S- specific
M- measurable
A-attainable
R- realistic and
T- timely.

S = SPECIFIC - Goals must be specific and written out. Goals that are not written out are less likely to be met. So, what is the difference between a dream and a goal? A dream remains in the mind and a goal is written down. Goal setting is more than simply scribbling down some ideas on a piece of paper. Your goals need to be thoughtfully completed and focused in reality. To write that you want to own a home is not a specific goal. Instead write down that the home you want is a 4 bedroom 3,300 square foot home on the beach. It has a boat launch for your watercrafts and a large infinity edge pool. There's an outdoor kitchen and a large 3 car garage. The wrap-around porch on the floor level has multiple rocking chairs and the widows walk on the second story has sliding glass doors that open up to the lounge chairs. The view of the water is unimpeded on all three sides, etc.

Does that sound more specific than saying you want to own a home? Can you envision that home? Now that's specific!

M = MEASURABLE - Goals must be measured for progress. Most managers will say, "If you can measure it you can manage it." I prefer, "If you can measure it, you can improve it."

In order to know if you're getting closer or further away from your goal you must be able to measure the results. As a child and well into my thirties I had the ability to gain and lose weight at will. I had no sympathy for those that struggled with weight issues. Then something happened in my mid forties. My metabolism changed, and I gained weight that I have had a hard time losing. Why didn't anyone warn me that I was turning into a big tub of goo? Because I would not have listened, that's why! So now I need to measure results on an incremental scale (pun intended) that I can manage and improve upon them. Think of your goals as measurements. Measurements are broken into smaller segments. A large goal must be broken down into smaller components.

One of the most difficult jobs for a sales person is prospecting. We'll cover alternative prospecting shortly, but for now let's consider this. Traditional Prospecting = every day you need to make so many prospecting calls to get so many appointments that will provide x number of proposals and lead to a set number of sales. Every sales person should know where they stand in their annual, quarterly, monthly, weekly and daily sales goals. To keep your pipeline full, you need to set aside a specific amount of time solely for prospecting activity. When prospecting falls off, sales inevitably follow. Measuring is critical to improving and/or changing your goals.

A = ATTAINABLE - Goals must be internalized if they are to be attainable - Goals that are inconsistent with your core values will most likely fail.

Throughout my career I have failed to meet sales goals and other times I have far exceeded and blown through the sales goals. The most important thing to remember about the goal is who set or created the goal and do I own it (have I internally accepted it as my own).

I once received an annual $250,000 revenue goal given to me by my manager. For those who don't know, that's a hefty middle market P&C insurance goal that very few meet. If the average commission on a product pays 10%, that equates to bringing $2,500,000 in premium to the agency. Most agent/producers will produce on average between $40,000 and $75,000 in new business revenue in a year. I internally knew that any producer that produced $150,000 in new business revenue would be viewed as a solid producer. One particular year I had only brought in $236,000 in revenue. Still, well above average and a respectable amount. Someone set the bar for me, they did not ask my opinion and therefore, I did not care one wit for obtaining a $250,000 goal. When the goal is not personalized, you will settle on a goal that you internally set, regardless of management. It's hard to attain a goal that you haven't truly bought into. When goals are set with the producer, they can truly let management know what's going on internally. However, when you dream big you succeed big.

"Attempt something so impossible that unless God is in it, it is doomed to failure." (Anonymous)

R = REALISTIC - your goals must be based in reality.
Unless you were fortunate to get a loan from Freddie Mac or Fannie Mae (when underwriting was non-existent), you are not going to apply to live in

a $1,000,000 home if you only make $40,000 in annual income. This is where management and sales people need honest and open communication. Many factors go into writing out your goals. When honesty and candor are present, truth will preside. Good managers exist to help you achieve your goals. Seek them out, ask for their advice and then get to work. If the manager you have is not a good fit for you, then try to find a seasoned professional and ask for their help. A mentor, among other things, is a coach or guide that will help point you in the right direction but will not micro-manage the process.

Does failure to meet a goal mean you are a failure personally? Heaven forbid! Not meeting a specific number in a quota has nothing to do with a person's value and self worth. A sales goal is only a number. Meeting it or exceeding it is also part of the learning process. If you don't meet the goal, then you have some choices to make.

1. Improve your work ethic/attitude.
2. Improve your sales skills.
3. Change the goal to a more realistic number.
4. Change employers/careers

The important thing to remember is that YOU set the real goal, not anyone else. Professionals overcome and adapt. Make your goals realistic and high enough for you to confirm within yourself that they are based on you giving one hundred percent effort. If you do that, more than likely, you will have surpassed the middle of the pack and perhaps even surprised yourself with the results.

T = TIMELY goals must be held to a time schedule and then broken down into smaller manageable components.

How do you eat an elephant? Answer - one bite at a time. When sales people are told to accomplish high goals it can be a very daunting task. When you get a few sales under your belt and have a book of business that's a great start to an occupation. When your pipeline is full and referrals are coming regularly, that's a great start to a career. Now when sales are scarce, new quotas are looming and the pipeline is empty, that's called fear and fear can inhibit action. Without action, you can't hit your goals. So what do you do? You perform tasks that you can measure in time. By breaking down a large task into smaller more manageable sections, you can accomplish large seemingly insurmountable goals. Progress comes with time. Unfortunately, most people don't recognize how many typical selling days are in a calendar year. Here's the formula 365 minus 104 (weekends) minus 8 (holidays) = 253 days in a sales person's calendar. This doesn't include vacations or sick time. Time is the only commodity we are all given an equal share of. How we use it, differs greatly with our productivity. In a sales person's schedule there are typically four crucial stages of time.

1. Sales Time - is done on the phone or in person. It is either prospecting time or selling time, period. This is where sales success begins, progresses and wins.
2. Service Time - visiting with clients to review stewardship plans, audits, claim reviews etc. This is when you schedule the follow up on the strategies you've discussed and planned.
3. Paperwork Time - done at night or in the morning after and before daytime working hours. Applications, non-crucial emails, planning and mailings.
4. Fun time - networking events, golf, fishing any client entertainment, meals, associations and going to the bank. Going to the bank includes cashing commission checks!
• If you had to guess, where do you think most successful sales people spend the bulk of their workday in?

If you guessed Sales Time, then you are correct. Consistent producers always have a goal. They have internal motivators that drive them to reach those goals. A goal is only a dream until you've internally motivated yourself to reach for it. The importance of goals and the initiative to act on them (action steps) is the discipline that winners have. Don't worry about how big your goals are, break them down into manageable segments (one bite at a time). Create an action plan and move forward making incremental progress. A sales career can be both scary and exciting and it is easier to measure progress when you first determine what it is you want. Don't wait, set your goals, write them down, and don't be afraid to dream big and have big goals!

"It must be born in mind that the tragedy of life doesn't lie in not reaching your goals but in having no goals to reach. It isn't a calamity to die with dreams unfulfilled but it is a calamity to not dream. It's not a disgrace not to reach for the stars; it's disgraceful to have no stars to reach for. Not failure, but low aim is sin."
Helmut Schmidt

Character

Professionals in all walks of life exhibit the similar traits of continuous study, training and improvement in their respective fields. They typically have a high degree of integrity, responsibility, a strong work ethic, and are internally motivated. In particular, sales professionals are curious by nature and know how to ask great questions and listen for needs. They are passionate about helping resolve problems and they are addicted to delivering on promises. Most handle rejection well and their resiliency and persistence typically make them goal driven. A successful sales career starts with character. Everyone has character, the question is, is it a good one or not? Dr. Martin Luther King Jr. said, "The ultimate measure of a person is not where they stand in moments of comfort and convenience, but where the stand in times of challenge and controversy." He believed that each man should be judged by the content of their character, not the color of their skin.

There are many great books written on how to refine ones character. Some of my favorite inspirational authors include: C.S. Lewis, John Maxwell, Zig Ziglar, Chuck Swindoll, Rick Warren, Coach John Wooden, Francis X. Maguire, Max Lucado, Ken Blanchard, Dale Carnegie, Tony Dungy Stephen Covey, Ravi Zacharias, Napoleon Hill and Van Eckern for his Speakers Source Book II filled with quotes.

While their works have influenced millions a simple alternative that has influenced billions (and the bestselling book of all time) is still, The Holy Bible. One only needs to read the Psalms and Proverbs to gain consistent insight into human nature. Everyone knows the Ten Commandments and the universal ethic of The Golden Rule ("Treat others as you would want to be treated in the same situation."). Living a moral lifestyle is a great start.

(Alternatively, starting a relationship with the Creator of the universe leads to a great life.)

Pat Summerall in his book, <u>Business Golf</u>, talks about, *"golfing naked."* He refers to how a person's true personality is revealed by the way they conduct themselves, (irrespective of how they are playing) on the golf course. Playing golf can be a challenging and frustrating game. The golf match can be the ultimate x-ray into the heart and soul of a man's character. For those that play the game this will ring true. A round of golf has many emotional ups and downs depending on how a player is performing. How you act on the golf course reveals a lot about how you act under pressure, react when winning and respond when falling short. We are all therefore "naked" on the golf course as to our core character. That's true for the sales professional too. We earn reputations by the way that we conduct ourselves with clients, colleagues and suppliers in the course of business.

Ralph Waldo Emerson had great insight when he said, *"Sow a thought and you reap an action; sow an act and you reap a habit; sow a habit and you reap a character; sow a character and you reap a destiny."* The fuel that you feed your mind (what you read, watch and study) will drive the engine of your ideas. What we focus our attention on we act upon and that creates momentum and establishes consistency. People that are consistent in their words and deeds become trusted and build reputations. Your good name is one of the most valuable assets you possess. Lose it, and you'll find it's extremely expensive and almost impossible to buy back. Treasure it at all costs.

People of character possess both integrity and intelligence. Integrity is telling the truth and keeping your word. It's doing the right thing even when nobody is looking. Intelligence is having a strong dose of intellectual curiosity. Curious people continue to grow (never confuse education with intelligence). Only after careful and honest reflection can one begin to work on their character. Once you've made the decision to change, then, give yourself a SWOT. The SWOT system was developed by Albert S. Humphrey at the Stanford Research Institute. SWOT stands for Strengths, Weaknesses, Opportunities and Threats.

- Strengths - what are my strongest assets, what do I offer that nobody else does?
- Weakness - what can be improved, what should I avoid and who can I lean on for help?
- Opportunities - what trends do I see, how can I help others meet their needs now?
- Threats - what's my greatest obstacle, what challenges can I turn into opportunities?

From time to time take a SWOT analysis of your character and your business. I am human and admit that sometimes I struggle to maintain a healthy positive outlook on life. It takes hard work and discipline to nurture and grow your character. The old Indian story about the two wolves brings the struggle to light.

One evening an old Cherokee told his grandson about a battle that goes on inside people. He said, "My son, the battle is between two "wolves" inside us all. One is evil. It is anger, envy, jealousy, sorrow, regret, greed, arrogance, self-pity, guilt, resentment, inferiority, lies, false pride, superiority, and ego. The other is good. It is joy, peace, love, hope, serenity, humility, kindness, benevolence, empathy, generosity, truth, compassion and faith." The grandson thought about it for a minute and then asked his grandfather: "Which wolf wins?" The old Cherokee simply replied, "The one you feed."

In my personal journey of refining my character I have relied heavily on my Christian faith. Hear me out and place your feelings about so-called

Christian leaders and societies on hold for just a second. We all agree that words have meaning. If I tell someone that I am a strict vegetarian and live the vegan lifestyle but I continually eat meat, fish and chicken, what would you think? Either I don't understand the definition of vegan or that I'm a liar. It's no different for us Christians. G.K. Chesterton said, "*The problem with Christianity is not that it has been tried and been found wanting, but that it has been found difficult and left untried.*" I always try to act in a manner honoring the principles exhibited by Jesus Christ. Of course, not being divine as He was, I'm going to make mistakes. After all, I'm only human. Daily discipline and study coupled with the reliance of the Holy Spirit to guide my thought life, matures me in my faith. Honestly, I don't understand how people cope through the trials of life without faith. I find it ironic that Frederich Nietzsche, one of history's biggest proponents of Atheism, basically said, "Whatever doesn't kill me makes me stronger." My faith sustains me and strengthens me. It allows me to see all the trials and problems in this life as fuel for my personal growth, maturity and refinement.

"*Consider it pure joy my brothers whenever you face trials of many kinds because you know that the testing of your faith develops perseverance. Perseverance must finish its work, so that you become mature and complete, lacking nothing. If any of you lacks wisdom, he should ask God, who gives generously to all without finding fault, and it will be given to him.*" (James 1:2-5 New International Version 1984)

"*The unexamined life is not worth living.*"
Socrates

"*You can easily judge the character of a man by how he treats those who can do nothing for him.*"
Johann Wolfgang von Goethe

Endurance

When you combine the self-discipline of persistence and resiliency you achieve endurance. Persistence pays off in the development of relationships over time. One of the hallmarks of the consultative process is determining if there is a fit. That's another way of saying - "Does it make sense to move your business at this time?" On one occasion I had prospected a large account and found that all of their insurance needs were being handled correctly. Their broker was doing a great job in all areas of service, marketing and coverage. I suggested that if there were ever a hiccup, I would like to be the first person they call. I also received permission to regularly follow up with and communicate with him. After three years of follow up calls, and emails and newsletters, there was a change in service with the incumbent broker and there was finally a fit.

- Are you persistent?
- Is persistence a state of mind?
- Can you teach yourself persistence?

Yes, and Yes! Many people fail in developing persistency because of "procrastination". I have a great chapter on procrastination and when I get around to writing it you can read it (cough). In the Star Wars saga, The Empire Strikes Back, Luke is with Yoda and he rushes off to save his friends in the Cloud City before he has completed his Jedi training. Yoda warns Luke that the Dark Side is a powerful foe. If he makes the decision to take one step down towards the dark side of the Force, that forever will it lead him into a path of destruction? It's the same with procrastination. Once you start to procrastinate it will lead to excuses, blame, indifference, neglect and failure. If you're there now, move away from the dark side, come back to the light and take action!

Developing persistency in two easy steps:

Step 1 - Purpose
The first step in developing persistence is defining what your purpose is. Know what you want and then taking the necessary steps to achieving that

goal. So many people want to be successful and yet they don't take the time to write down how they will achieve it. You can think about success all you want, but first you must write down specifically what it is you want and what you are willing to do to get it. Go ahead, get a pen, I'll wait.

Step 2 - Action
The second step to developing persistency is taking action. Focused action will develop your courage. Let's face it, sales is not for the timid, you have to have courage.

I remember walking into a meeting with an owner of a business, let's just say that he had a reputation for being ruthless with vendors. I had a spreadsheet containing five insurance companies and had highlighted the carrier I thought offered his company the best program for the premiums. He looked at me and said, "All you insurance agents are the same. All you want to do is put the most money in your pocket!" He told me to get out of his office and don't come back until I had something that was for his benefit! I left with my tail between my legs. At the end of the week I gathered my courage and came back to his office with another spreadsheet. I still had the same carrier I originally had highlighted and some additional options for comparison sakes. I sat down again and he said, "I told you, all you agents are trying to rip me off! Why don't you take this #@$*&, off my desk and don't come back!" I stood up and looked him dead in the eye and said, "Sir, my team has compiled the best program for you and your company that's in the marketplace. You wouldn't know a good deal if it hit you in the face!" He looked at me, smiled and said, "I was wondering if you were going to stand up for yourself, not many people will. Show me the one you think is the best and I'll have my secretary cut the check." I got the deal and eventually became close friends with him.

Attitude is the fuel for the engine of persistence. The basis of persistence is the power of the will. Napoleon Hill has written some of the best advice on persistence. He said, *"Will-power and desire, when properly combined, make an irresistible pair, and the lack of persistence is one of the major causes of failure."*

- Are you Resilient?

Resilience is someone that's had the wind knocked out of them, but they came back stronger and ran harder the next time. When I think of resilience I think of the movie hero, Rocky Balboa. Of all the Rocky movies, my favorite is still the first one, followed by Rocky 3. Throughout the Rocky saga, Rocky continuously faces obstacles, sets goals, is knocked down, gets back up and determines to overcome. For most of us this is difficult on our own. Thankfully, Rocky surrounded himself with friends and family. He had Adrian, Mick, Apollo, Pauly, Duke, and eventually, all of America. Cowboy wisdom says, *"Making it in life is like busting broncos. You're going to get thrown a lot, but the simple secret is to keep getting back on."* We all need support and if you are not fortunate to enlist three hundred million Americans to your cause like Rocky, let me share a few alternative steps that will help you become more resilient.

Step 1 - Starting your day
How do you start your day? Start your day in the right frame of mind. I start most days early in the morning with some quiet time. I read the Bible or an inspirational biography, I meditate, pray and have my devotions to recondition my mind. Whether you pray, read (newspaper doesn't count), meditate, exercise, it doesn't matter. Take the first part of your day to think. Think about everything you have to be grateful for. Think about your priorities, helping others, relationships. Early morning is best because it sets the tone for the day. Think about how many sunrises we are privileged to have within our lifetimes. How many have you seen in the past month? Focus you mind early first thing and the rest will follow.

Step 2 - Share
Do you share your goals, dreams and desires with trusted others. I've met with two friends almost every Friday for breakfast for the past fifteen years. We've supported each other in business and with our friendship. Start with two people you trust and respect. Ask them to meet for coffee once a week (you can never grow broke over breakfast meetings). The idea is to promote each other in whatever they are trying to accomplish in their business. There is wisdom and strength in the unity of ideas and

friendship. It's much easier to travel down the path of success with confirmation and guidance of trusted friends and supporters.

Step 3 - The Best Encouragement

Have you ever noticed the power of a few encouraging words from a friend and how they can revitalize you. Try it, if you know someone that could use encouragement, go see them or call them and let them know you're thinking of them (inquire about their business). Do NOT email or text them, make it personal. Better yet, find a way to support them by driving a referral to them. Let them know to expect a call or a visit from you with someone you just recommended to start using their services. New business referrals have a strange and wonderful way of encouraging most people. Helping others through encouragement will lift you and the other person up.

Step 4 - Remember

Lastly, look to those that have gone before you and been persistent. One of my favorite stories of persistence is in first book of the Bible (Genesis 37:1). It's the story of Joseph and the injustices he experienced as a young man. Eventually, God used those to fulfill a purpose and a destiny. Champions of persistency include great thinkers, generals, industrialists, survivors and saints. Biographies and stories that have inspired me include: Jesus, Dr. Martin Luther King Jr., Einstein, George Washington, John Adams, The Apostle Paul, R.U. Darby (Three Feet from Gold), King David, Abraham Lincoln, Edison, and Winston Churchill.

Reading their biographies and stories always includes chapters of their greatest moments of doubt and despair. These people persevered through tragedy to triumph. Read the stories of the men and women you respect and admire and learn from them, then write history for yourself and your family by becoming the hero in your lineage. Don't let a few small setbacks keep you from your goal. For that matter, don't even let big setbacks stop you from your mission. Remember, you may not reach all your goals, but striving for them will keep you well ahead of the masses that don't have any.

"Never give in, never, never, never, never, give up!"
Sir Winston Churchill's short commencement address

Setbacks

- What can we learn from failure?

We sales people are funny creatures. Sometimes we get emotionally involved in the sale and when we "fail" to close the deal we somehow think we are failures personally. Thankfully, no one experience completely defines us as people. People fail at performing tasks. Therefore failure is an *event* not a person! Just because someone doesn't meet a quota or close a sale, does not make them a failure as a person. We are human "beings," not human "doings." We get our self worth not because of what we do but because of who we are.

St. Francis de Sales said,

"Have patience with all things but first with yourself. Never confuse your mistakes with your value as a human being. You're a perfectly valuable, creative, worthwhile person simply because you exist. And no amount of triumphs or tribulations can ever change that. Unconditional self-acceptance is the core of a peaceful mind."

There is great power in encouragement! I firmly believe every person has a purpose. Just as timing has a lot to do with the outcome of a rain dance, we sometimes have difficulty in the ability to see past our present circumstances. Failure can be the foundation for greatness. The great preacher Chuck Swindoll, shares the abbreviated story of Abraham Lincoln in his book, Growing Strong in the Seasons of Life. It's a perfect example of a man who exhibited persistence, resilience, vision and who harnessed the impact of failure on his life.

He was born in 1809 in a log cabin in Hardin County Kentucky. His father was an illiterate wandering laborer, his mother a frail and sickly woman. They were forced out of their home when he was seven. His mother died when he was nine and he had virtually no formal schooling. His first attempted career in business in 1831 failed miserably. A year later in 1832 he ran for state legislature unsuccessfully. The same year he lost his job and applied to law school but was laughed out of consideration because of his miserable qualifications. Not long after that humiliating ordeal, he started a business with money he borrowed from a close friend. Before the year closed, however, that business failed and Lincoln claimed bankruptcy and spent the next 17 years paying off the debt. In 1835 he fell in love with Ann Rutledge, only to have his heart broken when she died soon after they were engaged.

In 1836 he had a complete nervous breakdown and spent six months in bed recovering. During 1838 he sought the speaker of the state legislature and was defeated. Two years later, he sought to become the elector of the state and was defeated. Three years later in 1843 he ran for congress and lost. In 1846 he ran for congress again and won but only two years later he ran for re-election and was soundly defeated. The year 1849 he sought the job of land officer in his home state but was rejected. He ran for Senate in 1854 and in 1858, losing both bids. In 1856 he sought the vice presidential nomination at his party's national convention and got less than one hundred votes, suffering another embarrassing defeat. Finally in 1860 Abraham Lincoln was elected 16th President of the United States and endured the most devastating war our country has ever experienced. His perseverance rewarded him with an unprecedented political success and he was elected to a 2nd term. Sadly, only 5 days after Lee surrendered on April 14 1865, Lincoln was assassinated before reaching 60 years of age. It was said of Lincoln by his biggest detractor, (Edwin Stanton -Secretary of War) "There lies the most perfect of man the world has ever seen... and now he belongs to the ages." Abraham Lincoln said, "When I left Springfield, I asked people to pray for me; I was not a Christian. When I buried my sons—the severest trial of my life—I was not a Christian. But when I went to Gettysburg, and saw the graves of thousands of our soldiers, I then and there consecrated myself to Christ." The biographer adds these lines to that moment— "The president was at the cross." In a final footnote the editor stated more eloquently than most that *"The steel of greatness is forged in the pit"*.

Hard times come in everyone's life, no one is immune. When they hit, you will have some difficult choices to make. You can choose to let life's disappointments defeat you, make you bitter or angry, keep you down and wallow in self pity. Or, you can choose the high way and let the circumstances of life mold you into an overachiever that turns tragedies into tomorrow's triumphs. Will you be bitter or better, the choice is yours. Experience can be a hard teacher because it gives the test first then the lessons. However, you too can be forged into steel by traveling through the pit.

Almost every insurance opportunity I have had involved the challenge of unseating the long term incumbent. On one occasion I was working on a very lucrative deal and I thought my chances were more than good as I had a few advantages in my favor.

1. I was in constant communication directly with the owner who was the decision maker.
2. I had just experienced some success having written a smaller piece of the business and had a foot in the door.
3. I had access to all the other markets, except the incumbent market.
4. The agency I worked for was the 5th largest brokerage in the country and had massive resources compared to the local small current independent broker.

The effective renewal date of the program was on a Thursday. I had all my numbers in from the underwriter ten days early from the renewal date and I knew I had two additional specific advantages.

- ✓ I was saving the insured a significant amount of premium in excess of $50,000 on the one line of coverage alone.
- ✓ I had approval from underwriting that improved the terms and conditions of the coverage with some additional endorsements that were not on the current program.

One week prior to the renewal I asked the owner when he was meeting with his current agent for the renewal. He said he would be meeting him on Tuesday morning and he would really like to see me on Monday afternoon. I recall having a marvelous weekend and had already been counting the commissions in my head. That Monday, my meeting went wonderful. The insured was pleasantly surprised to see the amount of savings and the improvements in coverage. He said he would probably call me tomorrow with the order to bind coverage. On Tuesday afternoon I called the insured and asked him how his meeting went with the incumbent. He said, the old incumbent (his long time friend) was shocked and saddened. He said he almost cried and that his numbers weren't even close. With a secret smile I then asked what the next step is. He said, "He needed a day for his incumbent to go back and see what he could come up with." That was surprise number one for me. Knowing the policy needed to be renewed by close of business on Wednesday for the Thursday 12:01AM effective date; I called his offices just before lunch. No reply. Left a message to call me and at 2:30PM still no reply. Finally got a call at 3:30PM from the owner and he told me some bad news. He said, his current agent took my information to his underwriters and they were willing to match my coverage and pricing in order to retain the business. As he was an old friend, the owner told me he was going to stay with his incumbent. After the shock wore off of losing what I thought was a slam dunk, I learned a few valuable lessons about accountability and the renewal process. Naturally, I wanted to ensure this from reoccurring in the future and I made the following changes to future sales cycles.

1. As you can guess, I failed to ask a simple pivotal question. If I had only said something like this, "Mr. prospect, suppose I come in with a great price and better terms and conditions regarding your insurance. Is it fair for me to suppose you would bind the coverage with me or are you going to take my information and pricing and hand it to your current broker to see if he/she can match it? The answer would have created my next steps.

2. In order to NOT become an unpaid consultant, if it makes sense, I may require my prospects to agree to sign a Non-Disclosure of Information notice (sample provided at the end of the book). This levels the playing field and prevents my information from slipping into the hands of the competition. Consider it trade secret protection. If they won't agree, then the words your prospect should hear are, "Next!" (Don't share my information!)

3. Provide prospects with enough value so that there is no need to enter into the bidding process. The Broker of Record (BOR) or Agent of Record (AOR) process will eliminate that and start the relationship. This is easier to say than to do and takes strategy and a relationship. (see Chapter 8 pg. 80 Alternatives to Bidding)

=

4. Consider holding one of their family member's hostages. Keep in mind this is risky because if it's a teenager they may not want them back and then you're stuck with a teenager (does a just kidding disclaimer even need to be added).

Unseating and addressing the incumbent (addressed in the PARC System) has to be dealt with and that takes courage and integrity from the sales person. Success and failure are great teachers, and like many of you, I've learned as much from, if not more from, my failures to close a sale, than from my successes. In sales, they are a necessary part of the process, because no one will close every sale, if that were possible then they wouldn't call it sales they would call it order taking. Everyone fails at something once in a while, that's why we sell professional liability Errors and Omissions (E&O) insurance (joking, hello).

"The way to accelerate your success is to double your failure rate."
Tom Watson

"Don't be discouraged by failure. Failure in a sense, is the highway to success because every discovery of what is false leads us to seek after what is true. And every fresh experience points out an error which we shall, afterwards, carefully avoid."
John Keats

For additional tips in preventing this sales scenario see page 101 The Paradox of the Liar

Last word about Setbacks, Disappointments & Changes

You thought we were done with this issue – there's so much more to understand. Sales people experience a lot of no's during the qualification process of eliminating suspects from prospects. My father used to say, rejection is always present at a school dance and in a sales career. Sales people develop thick skin and courage because they are always open to rejection.

Everyone wants to be liked but taking rejection in sales personally is a sure ticket to therapy. The professional must learn how to handle rejection well.

- When you are rejected how do you handle it?
- Have you ever met a person that wanted and welcomed trials and rejection?

Here are a few suggestions on how to handle rejection and change.

1. Knowing who you are as a person is pivotal. Do you <u>know</u> you have a purpose in life! That's a statement not a question.
2. Remember, to differentiate *who you are* from *what you do*. We are human beings, not human doings. What we do, does not determine who we are. We are all human beings made in the image of God. The important thing to remember is that when someone rejects your product or service they are not necessarily rejecting YOU (unless you're creepy).

3. To release the stress of rejection it's important to <u>possess a sense of humor</u>. People that have the ability to laugh at life will do well in a sales career. I don't think there has been an extended period of time where I have not had the opportunity to laugh.

I once received a letter in college from my parents concerning my youngest sister. In the letter, they explained that the family was traveling home from church on Sunday morning. They decided to cut through the back streets of the local community college on the drive home. My father said to my youngest sister, "Wow, look at all the seagulls in the parking lot. I wonder why they're not at the dump." My sister replied, "Dad, it's Sunday, the dump is closed." Needless to say, we still laugh at that story when we get together. The point is humor and laughter is the oil that eases the daily grind.

4. Focus on the benefits of rejection.

    a. The more we handle rejection the more we grow as people. Sure it's tough, but not impossible. Knowing that there's a purpose for your growth offers comfort. *"Trial by fire,"* is an old saying that speaks toward the painful experiences, troubles, problems and difficulties one must go through that tests a person patience, endurance or beliefs. Fire removes the dross and impurities of the metal.

Did you know:

✓   Walt Disney was fired by a newspaper editor because "He lacked imagination and had no good ideas." He went bankrupt several times before he built Disneyland. The park was also rejected by the city of Anaheim on the grounds that it would only attract riffraff.

✓   More than 30 Publishers rejected Dr. Seuss' first book, <u>To Think That I Saw It On Mulberry Street.</u>

✓   Henry Ford went bankrupt six times before he finally succeeded.

✓   The evaluation of Fred Astaire's first screen test: "Can't act. Can't sing. Balding. Can dance a little."

✓   Michael Jordan and Bob Cousy were both cut from their high school basketball teams.

✓   The movie Star Wars was rejected by every movie studio in Hollywood before 20th-Century Fox finally produced it. It went on to be one of the largest grossing movies in film history.

Keep failure in perspective, find comfort by looking towards others that have gone before you and experienced rejection. <u>Reminder</u>: Don't make major decisions after you've just experienced a major setback. Give it some time before you decide.

"Do not forsake wisdom, and she will protect you; love her, and she will watch over you. Wisdom is supreme; therefore get wisdom. Though it cost all you have, get understanding." (Proverbs 4:6-7 NIV)

    b. Substitute the word, "problem," with the word "opportunity." Again, this is your choice. We are all given the opportunity to use the circumstances of life as a learning platform. For those that subscribe to the American worldview, the problems of life are only minor speed bumps that slow us down momentarily before we can take off again.

5. The U.S. Marines preach, "Improvise, adapt and overcome!" This works just as well in sales boot-camp. Change happens so adapt and push forward. Life and sales do not go according to set plans sometimes. Numerous scenarios can change a business or a sale. Bumps can come from; unexpected health issues, natural disasters, economic uncertainty, crafty competitors, mergers and acquisitions (M&A), changes in leadership or underwriters to name a few. The professional must be flexible and prepare for unexpected twists and turns. Prepare your mindset first.

There's the old story of a junior banker who gets promoted to vice president. He approaches a senior executive and asks if he can ask her for some advice. The senior executive accepts. He said," What does it take to become successful?" The senior executive said, "That's easy, it comes from making smart decisions." The new vice president follows up with, "well what's the secret of making good decisions?" The senior executive responds, "Experience." The vice president finally asks how do you gain experience?" She replied, "By making wrong decisions."

I turn to the wisdom of Mark Twain when he said, "A man who carries a cat by the tail learns something he can learn in no other way."

Face it, everyone makes mistakes. That's how most of us grow. The wise person is the one who learns from those mistakes and takes action to never repeat the same ones twice.

Lastly, finding peace and stability inside will lend itself to your outside as well. It will help you when troubles arise or issues or concerns come (and they will come). Remember, whatever you are filled with will spill out when you are bumped.

- What fills you?
- What do you do to find peace and comfort?

There are very few of us who have made decisions we wouldn't change if we had known the results. However, if we are the sum total of our past choices, then, we should have few regrets and only new possibilities. Legitimate regrets should be limited, here's a few:

- ✓ Not spending enough time with your loved ones
- ✓ Being a workaholic (not to be confused with drive/ambition)
- ✓ Not taking a risk on something new (business, vacation, hobby)
- ✓ Not keeping in touch with friends
- ✓ Ignoring your health

It's absolutely true that we cannot change our past but it's equally true that we can affect our future! That's right, we are not victims of circumstance, we can change things now to impact what comes next. Forget the excuses, it's too late, it's too hard, there's no time, there's no money. Establish and prioritize what you need to change to avoid potential regrets. Then, take action towards accomplishing those goals. Every minute spent in preparation saves ten minutes in execution (don't look for the perfect time to act, **do it now**). Our lives change only when we change something we do every day. If we could kick the person that's responsible for most of our troubles, we wouldn't be able to sit down for a week. Living a life without regrets is very hard thing to do. It's because we are all prone to making mistakes. Regrets aren't about failures in accomplishing things, regrets happen when we don't put forth our best effort. Avoiding regrets is easy if we remember that we can't become what we need to be by remaining what we are.

"Now what should happen when you make a mistake is this: You take your knocks, you learn your lessons and then you move on. That's the healthiest way to deal with a problem." Ronald Reagan

"People often say that motivation doesn't last. Well, neither does bathing, that's why we recommend it daily." Zig Ziglar

"The ultimate measure of a man is not where he stands in moments of comfort and convenience but where he stands at times of challenge and controversy," Martin Luther King

"Some people come into your life as blessings. Some come into your life as lessons." Mother Theresa

"The 3 C's of life: Choices, Chances and Change - you must make a choice to take a chance or your life will never change." Anonymous

"All the adversity I've had in my life, all my troubles and obstacles, have strengthened me... You may not realize it when it happens, but a kick in the teeth may be the best thing in the world for you." Walt Disney

Keep a Journal!

Successful people learn as much from their mistakes as they do from their successes. Journaling is an important tool for keeping track of where you've been and what has taken place to get where you are today. No one has a perfect memory (unless you're a mom). Memories tend to fade so writing down your daily experiences, both the trials and the achievements, will help you immensely. Incremental steps forward, (coupled inevitably with a few steps back) continuously move me in the direction I want to go. Often when I reread how I was feeling in the moment it helps me to remember it's not a race but a journey.

- Do you document your wins and losses?
- Do you refer back to them on a consistent basis to benefit from your experiences?
- Do you keep a record of what works and what doesn't work for you?
- Would you be able to write an inspiring book on your experiences and how you overcame setbacks when the year is over?

It's vitally necessary that you learn from each sales call and develop your strengths and your style. The high road is always more difficult. Every individual that has been labeled successful will tell you that they've been through highs and lows. As an optimist I find it hard sometimes to remember my mistakes or I convince myself that this time it will be different. Referring back to my journal refocuses lessons that should not be soon forgotten. When I look back at my journal I also find the feelings I had been experiencing "in the moment" eventually changed. It's a great reminder that usually, everything works out. Whether it's painful, joyous, or scary, your emotions written down and the lessons you learn are taken more seriously when they've come from your own hand. Remember, failures are not fatal, they're launching pads.

"Never give up, Never surrender!"
Mathesar, from the movie Galaxy Quest

PART II

Chapter 4

Questioning Skills

From the time my children first attended elementary school as small children until they graduated from middle school, I don't think there was a day that went by that I didn't begin our conversations with, "Did you ask any good questions today?" They realized at an early age that having an inquisitive mind is critical to growing as a person and confirming truth. I wanted them to know that ideas have consequences. Some things in life are right and others are wrong regardless of opinion. As a daily habit, it challenged them to think logically and communicate effectively.

All sales people know that there are two general types of questions. There are **Closed Ended** – Questions that elicit yes or no answers.

- Is that a fair price?
- Were you expecting that result?
- Do you like my hair?

Open-Ended – Questions that require more descriptive answer not just a yes or no.

- Why is that important to you?
- How did that happen?
- Can you share?
- Could you tell me more about..?

Because open ended question require lengthy descriptive answer, they are assumed to be more powerful. Unless you are training a dog, this is typically true. Good questioning can bring insight into a situation. For instance:

When my youngest son was about 7 years old he asked my wife, "Mommy, does our town have a superhero? My wife was puzzled and replied, "What do you mean?" He said, "Well, Gotham City has Batman and Metropolis has Superman, does our town have a Superhero?" My wife quickly thought through the question and with wisdom said, "You know, we don't have a super hero, so why don't YOU be the superhero for our town?" Placing his little hands on both hips he said, "Well that's a little hard to do when you won't even let me past the top of our own street!" Here are my:

Top 10 benefits of asking great questions:

1. Gain information – who, what, when, where, how
2. Clear up fuzzy thinking (clarify) – Are you sure you know what you're doing?
3. Reduce mistakes – Would it help if I got out and pushed?
4. Prevent objections – Would it kill you to try this?
5. Defuse volatile situations – Who's in charge?
6. Reduce anxiety – What's the worst that could happen?
7. Uncover pain – Does this hurt?
8. Open lines of communication – Who do you think you are?
9. Take the sting out of criticism – Can we talk?
10. Motivate and persuade – Who cut your hair a blind man with hiccups?

Sales professionals rely on questioning skills for success. They are the keys to unlocking the needs of a prospect. Most new sales people soon discover that better questioning techniques can help avoid four common stumbling blocks in the sales cycle.

1) **Didn't ask** the appropriate questions (uncover their needs)
2) **Didn't understand** why they were buying (their buying motives)
3) **Didn't clarify** the next steps in the process (mutual mystification)
4) **Felt uneasy** about being combative (crossing the line) with the prospect

Many books on sales typically ask the reader to, "Come up with a series of thought provoking and intelligent questions to ask the prospect that your competition is not asking." I agree, developing great questions is one of the most critical skills you can master. However, these materials would:

    A. Rarely provide specific examples pertinent to my industry.
    B. Failed to explain in what order to ask the questions.
    C. Did not explain how to ask the question.

In sales, *how* you ask a question is just as important as *what* you ask. There's a huge difference in the tone of a question when the goal is to gain understanding versus simply challenging a person's viewpoint. Have you ever tried asking a simple question in an honest inquisitive tone such as, "How did you arrive at that conclusion?" Typically, once you understand a person's viewpoint (worldview) you can start a conversation. Remember, *how* you do what you do is just as important as *what* you do. All insincerity or manipulation techniques must always be avoided (that's why we tackled character development in the PALACES first).

The order of your questions will be addressed when we discuss introductions. The specific examples are within the PARC system - hold your horses, almost there, keep reading.

"What's another word for thesaurus?"
"Do Lipton employees take coffee breaks?"
"Why doesn't Tarzan have a beard?"
Questions from comedienne Steven Wright

"There is no stupid question. Stupid people don't ask questions."
Anonymous

Chapter 5

Qualifying a prospect

After you've identified an opportunity you need to qualify it to determine if whether or not it will be a good fit. That's political correct speech for "so you don't waste you or your team's time, energy and money." In the insurance field, a good fit is a three way win. When you place business as an insurance broker it has to be a win for the carrier, a win for the client and a win for you. Winning is about finding and delivering what's best for all parties involved.

Qualified prospects share distinct characteristics.

1. Aware of and have a need for your service

2. Trust you and/or your company

3. Willingness to listen to you and start a relationship

4. Have a sense of urgency

5. Ability and authority to pay/purchase

How many accounts have you tried to throw up against the wall, hoped that they stuck, only to end up being a "quote and information" machine? Stop wasting yours and your team's time. Part of winning more business is directly related to our qualifying skills. Most prospects will not volunteer the real reasons for their objections. Therefore, good questioning skills are important in determining if the prospect is truly qualified. Those discovery questions are dealt with in the PARC System subjects (on the very next pg. - thank you for being patient).

Let's try winning and see what it feels like. If we don't like it, we can go back to our traditions." Paul Tsongas

"If winning isn't everything, then why do they keep score?"
Vince Lombardi

Chapter 6
The PARC Method of Discovery

If the scariest three letters in the alphabet are IRS then perhaps the scariest two letters are M&A. With mergers and acquisitions can come uncertainty and fear. However, fear, translated into adversity, can also lead to great opportunity. And so it happened to me. The merger and acquisition of my former employer allowed me to verbalize a system I developed decades ago and is the driving concept behind Donovan Insurance Solutions consultative brokerage. It happened like this.......

Upon the merger, both teams of brokers were asked to participate in sales training classes. Ultimately, I found myself sitting in a training class among my former competitors, now my new colleagues. And, oh yes, they reminded us, who, bought who! The proctor for the course had just taken us down the sales funnel and had asked each of us to come up with specific questions that pertained to each segment of the funnel. For those that are not familiar with The Sales Funnel, it is a systematic approach whereby the sales person brings the prospect down an ever tightening circle from first call to closing the deal. They accomplish this by moving from:

- Initial contact
- Building rapport
- Qualifying by identifying needs
- Proposal
- Negotiations
- Closing the sale

Permit me to pause. Typically, my attitude is to continue to grow daily and learn something new that I can apply into my own style of selling in order to improve. However, on this occasion I admit, I was a little bored by some of the basics being discussed and I was not paying close attention. To my surprise, my moment of truth came and I was randomly called upon by the class proctor, to give an example of a question we were to have been working on. Being caught off guard, (and sensing management's eyes upon me) I said with all honesty, "I'm sorry, I have squat, I have nothing." A little stunned by my candor, she asked me why that was, and how exactly did I sell? Now there are moments in life that each of us look back upon and can vividly recall the scene. This was one of those times of clarity. Ironically, up until this point, I don't ever recall anyone ever asking me this very question about how it is that I actually sold. Thinking quickly and honestly, I responded that I had a grid in my mind on every sales call where I asked the prospect what they were trying to <u>fix</u>, <u>accomplish</u> or <u>avoid</u> in the areas of their insurance needs. I said, "In my experience, there are only eight possible areas of pains that exist for those that have insurance.. It's an acronym I use to help me stay on track and it's, PARRRCCC or simply **PARC**." She asked me what PARC was and I took a deep breath and continued saying, "It's all about the prospects priorities:

Premiums – Everyone wants a fair price so what strategies are they employing to keep their costs as low as possible for the highest value?
Accountability - How do they hold their current broker accountable?
Renewals - How valuable would it be to receive their renewals weeks beforehand?
Resources - What resources are they receiving now, how's it working? How much has it directly impacted their bottom line since implementation?
Relationship - what's the relationship with their incumbent broker like and are they willing to break it if we can add value and resolve their situation?
Claims - What's their experience been? What steps have been taken to remove those claims that are on the books now and what's their process for future prevention?
Coverage - When's the last time they had a forensic coverage audit?
Communication - How often and in what manner do they wish to be communicated with? When was the last time they had their current client service agreement reviewed?

I rattled this entire speech off in about a minute. The picture I still have in my mind was her open mouth shocked look of silence. She finally said, "That is brilliant, do you mind if I use that?" I said, "Sure, why not." I had avoided embarrassment, proven a modicum of competency and was left alone for the remainder of the sessions. That was the first time I had explained the PARC method to others. It is an idea and method I had been using for years and had finally verbalized it in a simple and succinct moment.

As I used this system for identifying needs, I have come up with variations to the questions within each category. These questions are guidelines, so feel free to create your own. Practice, experiment and customize your questions according to your style. You'll find that stepping out of your comfort zone will open up new opportunities.

A quick note about a prospect's priorities

Every business has them and they are as diverse and different as shells on a beach. Figuring out a company's priorities is critical to understanding if there's a potential business fit.

- What was your greatest accomplishment last year and what do you see will be this years?
- Can you share with me the major challenge your company is facing this year? Is that an industry wide problem or specific to your company?
- What is it you're trying to accomplish this year?
- What kind of concerns do you have with this project?
- Why is that the greatest concern?
- How are you approaching it?
- Can you give me an example of what you're talking about?
- Given what you're doing now, is there any room for improvement?
- Let's suppose we could fix these problems, tell me what the perfect results look like six months from now?
- When I say P&C insurance, what one word comes to mind?
- Where do you feel you need the most help?
- As the CEO/CFO, what one thing keeps you up at night?

Develop questions that get to the heart of their main concerns. You will be surprised how many great answers are out there that go unasked.

Premiums

Premiums are a major component of the total cost of risk for a client. Typically a businesses' total cost of risk (TCOR) is comprised of risk management costs, administration costs, premiums, claims costs, downtime, rehiring, training, lost bids losses, deductibles/retention levels, premiums, administration costs etc.etc.

- When you added up your companies total cost of risk, what did that amount to?
- When you analyzed the total cost of risk what was that number?
- What specific strategies were provided for you to help you squeeze the most out of your insurance budget? How are they working?
- When you sat down and met with the company underwriter to discuss how you are different from similar looking risks, what was the conversation like?
- Did you notice anything strange or any discrepancies in rating your risk when you were reviewing the underwriter's notes in the marketing file?
- Typically when we talk with the decision makers we always hear about the importance of cash flow. Cash flow is King is the mantra. During your premium audits have you ever received credit back from the carrier or had to pay additional premiums?
- What kind of credits are you receiving now?

Remember, premiums are only a part of their TCOR. Remind your prospect that costs (not just premiums) are what you are focused on reducing. Be clear, be confident and consistent.

"People will pay a fair price for their insurance coverage when value is justified."
Paul Donovan

Accountability

Customer Service contracts outline all of the services that a broker will perform during the year. It lists the service team, their responsibilities and time frames with which to accomplish agreed upon goals.

- Who is your current broker and how long have you been with them?
- How often do you meet with your broker now?
- Can I review a copy of your customer service agreement, to see if there's anything that might be missing?
- How do you hold your current broker accountable?
- Can I review a copy of last year's stewardship report that you received?
- How much did you pay your broker last year?
- Was that through commissions or consulting/service fees?
- Did that include contingency fees?
- What's your process for making decisions like this?

For a sample copy of a customer service contract please see the appendix at the end of the book.

"When brokers take the initiative to be transparent with their clients, relationships of trust get established."
Paul Donovan

Resources

Proper application of resources is a significant risk management tool, and can directly impact the costs of a business and its insurance program. Costs include the total cost of risk for an account - premiums, claims, administrative time, employee training etc.

- What type of resources is your broker providing for you now?
- How are those resources performing?
- When you measured how much profit (return on investment ROI) those resources have brought to the bottom line, were you satisfied with that number?

- Do you have a full time risk manager?
- Questions can be developed around the following types of resources:

Stewardship Reports	Risk Management portals
OSHA compliance	Work Comp audits
TPA Services	Safety Meetings/incentives
Cost containment	In-house claims
ADA Compliance	Contract reviews
Contingency Planning	Employee Communications
Modifier verifications	Return to work programs
Loss Controls	

Developing questions is all about services that you offer that can add value and save costs for the prospect.

What do you think - Who's to blame for the lack of trust in most politicians? Sure, we can blame the hypocrisy, unfulfilled campaign promises and the normal moral decline. Then again, we should blame ourselves. Long-term memories are non-existent during elections. The same can be said of our clients! That's right. Clients tend to have amnesia when things are going smooth. They will also forget that their trusted advisor (that would be you) had anything to do with the good times, if you don't remind them. Careful analysis of an account's PARC System pain points allows identification and allocation of resources that can best help a client's TCOR. Applying resources is a process. It is critically important that you monitor progress in the reduction of costs over time. The reduction in TCOR and your added value to the client's business has a dollar value. It is vital that you regularly report those results to the client. Regularly reporting results over time will justify your recommendations and value to the client. Routinely communicate, promote and prove your value with an annual Stewardship Report. Relationships built on friendship are worthy, relationships built on value are unbreakable by competitors.

"Trusted advisors are purveyors of resources, NOT vendors."
Paul Donovan

Renewals

There are a few reasons why agents are typically late in delivering a renewal to their insured. Many times it has nothing to do with laziness from the underwriters or a late submission process. The main reason is that the incumbent agent is afraid that an early renewal in the hands of their client would allow the client time to seek out alternatives from other brokers. Price then becomes the main factor because no relationship or additional value was established.

- What's your typical renewal process like now? Are you comfortable with that?
- How valuable would it be to you to receive your policy renewals 3-4 weeks ahead of time?
- How important is it to have all your policy effective dates concurrent?
- Does it make sense to have all your policies come due at the same time so that you only have to concentrate on your insurance program renewal, one time per year?
- (for FL and susceptible areas) Knowing that hurricane season is between June 1 - November 30, is there a reason you are renewing inside of two hurricane cycles for your property during that time?
- Do you think it might benefit you to move your effective dates out of hurricane season/away from some of the more popular dates 1/1, 4/1, 7/1 so that you can receive more attention from underwriting?
- The majority of reinsurance contracts come due on 1/1 as well as a vast number of insured businesses. Would it make sense to move your effective date to an alternative date so that you would receive more favorable review of your risk by underwriters?

"Renewals will continue to be a major thorn in the side of the client until brokers decide that their relationships are secure enough to weather the competition."
Paul Donovan

Relationships

There's always an incumbent agent to unseat. Your competitor already has some type of relationship. Unless you're working with a new start up business (and those are rare) there will already be insurance in place. You are either going to be taking business from someone or losing it to someone. That's right; your competition is always at the door vying for your client and ultimately, your income. Until you identify the strength or weakness of the relationship the prospect has with the incumbent, determining next steps in the process will remain questionable at best.

- When working with a new partner what are some of the biggest mistakes that are made (what frustrates you)?
- What are your expectations from our relationship moving forwards?
- In your opinion, what does the perfect relationship with a broker look like?
- Let's suppose for a minute that we could fix these problems, tell me what the perfect results look like in 6-9 months?
- What will define a successful outcome for you?
- What made you decide to work with your current broker?

When dealing with the decision maker try these
- What's your time frame for achieving this?
- In addition to yourself, who else is involved in the decision process?
- What have you already seen that has particularly appealed to you?
- How will you know you've made the right decision?

The PARC method helped transition my thinking from salesman-centric to client-centric. Too many agents and brokers fail to properly discern this vital connection and unfortunately, end up becoming unpaid consultants by entering the bidding war. Try phrasing your question like this when the incumbent agent has a long term solid relationship:

- Mr. Prospect, I understand that you have a relationship with your broker. I truly appreciate that type of loyalty in my clients as well. We have a couple of options:

a. I can keep in contact with you until things change in your current relationship or there's a hiccup in your services. In that case, I would then want to be the first person you call.

b. You can decide that there is absolutely nothing that would break your current relationship. In that case, I will no longer waste your time.

c. There's a possibility that there are some areas where you believe there could be some improvement in your services, and perhaps I just haven't asked the right question or listened intently enough. Which of these three categories do you think best fits our situation today?

Complete honesty and sincerity typically wins the day. We will discuss in further detail the absurd notion that, a prospect may not tell the complete truth to the sales person, later in the book under the title The Paradox of the Liar - pg. 95.

"Do unto others as they do unto you. Plus 10 percent."
Henry Kissinger

"Money cannot buy peace of mind. It cannot heal ruptured relationships, or build meaning into a life that has none."
Richard M. DeVos

Claims

Claims is the one area that directly proves the broker's promise. Most insured's want only two answers. <u>How much</u> am I going to collect and <u>when</u> will the check be in their hands. It is the job of the broker to clearly communicate and work in conjunction with the adjusters to expedite the process.

- What's been your experience with claims over the past 3 years?
- What kind of claims have you had in the past 3 years?
- Is that a severity issue or a frequency issue?
- What have you done to resolve those? How's it working? Are you receiving the results you had hoped for?
- When you measured the impact of claims to your costs, what was the impact?
- Are your claims handled by the carrier reps or does your broker have internal claims reps that guide the process?
- How does your broker help you with claims now?
- Not all carriers treat claims the same, have you ever suspected any fraudulent claims? (retail calls it shrinkage)
- What protocols are in place to identify and fight unjustified fraudulent claims?
- Questions can be developed around the following claims information
    1. Direct costs = the claim cost, attorney fees and administration fees.
    2. Indirect costs = loss of productivity, worker replacement, supervisor training, administration
    3. Auto = potential loss of a client/customer because of down time.
    4. Property = cost of replacement or function

Questions to the prospect should revolve around strategies that he/she may or may not be implementing. In some instances, a strategy to save a client money, involves negotiating terms and conditions of claims payment up-front with the underwriters and adjusters. In many liability claims, the insurance carrier typically reserves the right to pay nuisance small claims as they see fit. A question you could ask a prospect might be:

- Have you ever had any smaller claims that the carrier paid without consulting you first? Have you ever considered setting up a contract with the carrier that clarifies, "before the carrier can issue a check for claims over $7,500, the carrier must contact the broker and the insured to discuss why the claim should be paid versus litigation."

Since claims impact loss ratios and in turn affects premiums on renewal, questions about claims are limitless. Loss controls, surveillance, anti-fraud considerations, litigation costs, OSHA compliance, and potential awards or judgements are just some of the areas of concern.

For workers compensation claims there are many claims saving tips that will directly impact the employer's premiums. One potential question:

- As you know, indemnity payment to the employee severely impacts your Work Comp modifier. Have you ever considered paying the indemnity portion directly to the employee in order to limit the impact on your mod? Has that strategy ever been discussed? Why not?

Serious claims review should take place regularly until the claim is closed. Claims prevention is just as important as claims resolution in its impact on a client's insurance premiums, terms and conditions. Ask good questions.

"There are only two types of companies, "Those that have claims and those that are going to have claims."
Unknown

"My recent car accident was far less traumatic than dealing with my insurance company over the claim process."
Anonymous

Coverage

It's been said that lawyers typically are taught to never ask a question that they already don't know the answer to. It's a great way to avoid surprise answers. Likewise, asking prospects questions that you have a high probability of knowing the answer is a fair technique with one important caveat. Most important: If I ask a question about a service that I don't think the prospect is receiving, I had better be able to offer that service.

Another great way to improve your coverage questions is when you dedicate yourself to becoming an expert in a niche market.

- When you had your last coverage audit did you find any overlaps where you were paying for duplicate coverage?
- Were there any surprises where there was a "gap" in coverage you thought you had?
- What types of coverage are you currently self insuring for (flood, high deductibles, wind etc.)
- When did you have your last appraisal for all your property values? Was there any potential for co-insurance penalties?
- What recommendations did your current broker make about your coverage the last time you met?
- Have you ever discussed the differences between: Actual Cash Value (ACV), Replacement Cost (RC), Agreed Value and/or Functional Replacement Cost?
- Have you ever had premium returned to you or been billed at audit? How important is cash flow? Have you discussed strategies to resolve?

There are hundreds of ways to cut costs in insurance coverage. Gauging the client's appetite for risk, access to markets/relationships and a host of other factors come into play. At time of claim, most insured's don't want to profit off of calamity, they only want to be made whole again. Focus on making the client whole by asking what's most important to them, at a fair price and don't forget to document your discussions with the client (have them sign off on the conversation details).

"People who take risks are the people you'll lose against." John Sculley

Communication

If it costs more to get a new client than to keep a current one, then why would a broker neglect a current client after they are on the books? It seldom happens right? Regular and constant communication with clients is important for retention, referrals, branding, marketing and overall relationship development. Contacting a client without relevant information to risk or business opportunities is a rarity in the insurance industry as it is always in constant state of change. Meeting expectations with *proactive* communication is the key.

- How often do you (want to) meet with your broker?
- What is the preferred method of communication with your company? When we correspond, who is required to be cc'd on information?
- When you receive your Stewardship Report at the end of the year does it meet your expectations?
- Can we review your Customer Service Contract?
- What is the longest acceptable time for return calls before you would feel alienated?
- Is instant on-line access to your policy information important?
- How much of a difference would on-line training and risk management availability make to you?

When you ask these questions you inevitably will have some prospects give you the deer in the headlights look. That's OK. If you and your agency are willing to step up and provide this level of service, you have further differentiated yourself without directly disparaging the competition. To be honest, your competition is probably doing these things now and if they are not, they will be soon. Remember, never bad-mouth your competition. When you throw mud at others, not only do you get your hands dirty, but you lose some ground as well.

When you need clarification or want more details try following up with:

- Can you tell me more about that, please?

- Can you help me understand that better, please
- Can you give me an example?
- I'm curious, why do you do it that way?
- How's that working?

Additional Power Questions
- What do you look for?
- What have you found?
- How do you propose?
- What's been your experience?
- What do you like about?
- What's the deciding factor?
- How have you successfully used?
- What makes you choose?
- How do your customers react to?

Miscommunication or the lack of communication, has been the cause of many a conflict. Typically, when I want to relay a critical concept I take my lessons from the masters. Great communicators relay stories, parables and illustrations to make their point (everyone has a story). Think about the great lessons you have learned in your personal and business life. Try to relay that message via a story to impact your main point. Your audience can empathize with similar experiences brought to life through a story.

The Strategy of the FAA (not the Federal Aviation Administration)

The first universal truth in sales we said was trust. The second universal truth in sales is; the fastest easiest way to discover the needs of a prospect, starts with asking what their trying to Fix, Accomplish or Avoid. Regrettably, some prospects sometimes don't even know the answer to that simple question.

On one occasion I was sitting with a CEO and his corporate attorney for lunch. Their company had huge property values nearing a billion dollars. After enjoying our meal we were drinking coffee and I finally got down to business. I asked, "So, who do you work with on your P&C insurance?"

He said, "Oh, we've been with our broker (One of the top 5 firms in the U.S.) for over 10 years. He's based out of New York City and we love him." I said, I completely understand, in fact, I too enjoy that level of loyalty from my clients and those relationships are hard to break and great to have." I continued, "I'm curious, can I ask when your policies come up for renewal?" He very quickly said, "As a matter of fact, our renewals take place in a few months, I think in mid-October." "Hmmm," I said. "Is there a reason why you would renew your policies at the height of Hurricane season and potentially be in jeopardy of non-renewal or at best higher premiums? I continued. "I typically steer my high valued clients out of renewing inside of two hurricane renewal cycles and potentially not get the appropriate look from underwriters?" Then I shut up. The CEO looked at his attorney and then he said, "You know, that is a very valid point, would you mind coming by my office later to pick up our information and further discuss some strategies." Knowing what to ask takes experience and knowledge of potential problems/pains that your prospects all have (PARC). Knowing when to ask it and how to ask just takes practice, awareness and prayer. Remember the famous billboard that read, "As long as there are math tests in school, there will always be prayer in school." Awareness reminds me to pray for wisdom and timing. Consider only two actions when you encounter a solid relationship or dissatisfaction.

1. When the prospect and their incumbent agent have a solid long term relationship that you are not going to break short-term. Ask permission to stay in contact at least a couple of times per year and let them know that you want to be the first person they call when the hiccup occurs. Move on to another prospect. Next.

2. When you've uncovered an area of pain in the PARC system, and it's enough discomfort that will allow the next steps of the process to occur. Set firm next steps and expectations for action, moving the sales process forward.

The PARC areas of "pain" were a major breakthrough for me and offered an easy track to run on when in the discovery phase with a prospect. First, identify potential problems or areas of concerns and if unsure, ask someone with experience for help.

- Mr. Prospect, in my experience, typically I ask potential clients what they are trying to fix, accomplish or avoid in the following areas PARC. Perhaps you're having problems or a concern about one of those areas? Why don't you tell me what matters most to you/concerns you most.

To help you remember, put your category of issues into an acronym and filter them through the FAA. If you want to be a pro, ask about the consequences or effects of a problem, difficulty or dissatisfaction. Think like a business owner when developing your questions and think, *What would happen if...?"*. Could this problem affect future profitability or what effect could this have on customer satisfaction if not resolved? Could that lead to added costs? What affect do these problems have on competitive position? **Remember – good questions won't jump into your head when you're on the call so do your homework!**

Asking FAA questions will help you determine if there is a fit between what you offer and what they're looking for. Great questions about their PARC concerns can easily be adapted to any sales person's personal style. As you experiment and try new questions with prospects you will inevitably discover which ones work best for you.

"Successful people ask better questions, and as a result, they get better answers."
Tony Robbins

"I never learn anything talking. I only learn things when I ask questions."
Lou Holtz

PART III

Chapter 7
Essentials of the Insurance Professional
Why People Buy

- Have you ever asked your customers why they purchased from you?
- Do you know or do you just think you know?
- If you want to replicate success doesn't it make sense to discover why it is that a person bought from you?

In school they taught us that in order to reach a reasonable decision; we should measure the weight of evidence, based on facts and then logically come to a conclusion. If we were to follow this line of decision making, then the least expensive and best quality service or merchandise would always win. This process does not hold true in sales. Most sales are made because of buying motives and through added value brought by the purchase. Ask yourself:

- When you shop, what makes you purchase something?
- How much does price and quality come in to play?
- Do you purchase logically or emotionally?

<u>Buying motives</u>

Motives are emotional in nature and not merely based on the quality of a product or the services provided. Experience tells us, it's not always based on the least expensive product. I can hear all of you yelling (southerners translation = y'all), Paul, what are you talking about, I don't even know what a buying motive is? Buying motives are drives or urges that an individual seeks to satisfy.

Top 7 Reasons People Buy

1. Desire for gain.
2. Freedom from "fear of loss."

3. Recognition.
4. Emotional satisfaction (attraction, love of others).
5. Comfort and convenience.
6. Security and protection.
7. Health.

Many sales people fail to take into account the buyer's reason(s) for the purchase.

Top 7 Reasons Sales are Lost

1. Did not clearly identify needs of the prospect.
2. Your service or product could not appropriately resolve prospects needs.
3. Did not meet with the decision maker.
4. Did not determine relationship with the incumbent.
5. Did not provide enough value.
6. Could not meet time frame.
7. The prospect did not like you or your organization (no rapport).

WAIT - isn't there going to be anything about price, you ask? No! People will pay a higher price for value in more expensive *valued* sales. If price was the main motivator for sales then Lexus, Mercedes, BMW and Cadillac would be out of business. It's our job to find out how the prospect perceives value and then how we can deliver that value, better than the competition.

Once I left a prospect's office with the commitment for next steps. We agreed that we would perform a forensic audit on their insurance coverage. A coverage audit typically reviews all the limits, terms, conditions endorsements and exclusions in an insurance contract. The concentration is to identify the client's concerns and then, look for overlaps or gaps in important coverage. During our meeting the prospect was constantly focused on our ability to save him premium dollars. His mantra was price, price, price! After we had our results we made another appointment to share our findings. We found that his property limits were well undervalued and that he was in danger of violating some co-insurance penalties in the event of a claim. By having examples of common claims for him to review, we showed exactly how much he would be receiving with respect to different claims scenarios. We also shared supporting appraisal data and important gaps that could be resolved by adding some key endorsements. The net result was going to cost this prospect approximately $38,000 more in annual premium. All our competitors, including his current agent, came in with reduced rates and coverage. He thanked us for our work and within a week we were appointed his new broker. Value for this client was about protecting his business that he had worked a lifetime to build. How did we know that? We asked, "What are the key priorities of the insurance program and what keeps him up at night?" If we had followed the typical broker activity of "Quote my program just like I have it now." Then, we would have been copying someone else's mistake. Finding the decision makers hot button, (what do they value most) and then meeting those expectations and resolving their issues provided value. Whether you sell a product or a service, the sale is always about the perceived value of the prospect.

A great exercise to perform is to candidly ask your last five sales, why they actually purchased from you? I bet some of you will be surprised at their answers. It may have had nothing to do with the reasons why you thought they bought. *Sales are always about the perceived value of the prospect.* Value can come in many forms. It can be convenience, speed, capacity, competence, reputation, relationship, security or a host of other benefits. People will pay for value, but they will balk at paying, when value has not been established. If you rely on price alone, you will eventually lose on price alone.

❖ There's no designated rant area so I'm creating it here. **Paul's RANT Area** - My rant concerns the word, "kindness." It's true, that most people purchase from people that are *most like them* and/or from *people that they like*. Therefore, you had better be at a minimum, one of the two. Kindness is one of the most underrated traits in an individual and in an organization. There are those in business that think the only way to get ahead is to make sure somebody else loses. They manage with intimidation and fear. What a corrupt and crazy way to think! I'm not naiveté, but I guarantee, people are more productive in an encouraging atmosphere rather than one based in fear or anger. Look at the success, respect and admiration of a coach like Tony Dungy and you will get the idea. He is always reasonable and in control. He harnesses his emotions and attacks the issue or behavior and not the character of the person. When someone makes a mistake, be kind. When someone is having a bad day, be kind. When you need to fire someone, be kind. Life is filled with teachable moments, be kind.

The more expensive the purchase, the more emotional the purchase becomes. Smaller transactional type sales do tend to rely more on price as a determining factor. Keep in mind, everyone's threshold and definition of "expensive," is different. That's why some people don't blink at a $100,000 premium where others get anxious over a $35 increase in premiums. Most business professionals understand this difference and they are willing to pay for value.

"I speak two languages, Body and English"
Mae West

"I have always said that everyone is in sales. Maybe you don't hold the title of salesperson, but if the business you are in requires you to deal with people, you, my friend, are in sales."
Zig Ziglar

Chapter 8
Alternatives to Bidding and Choosing a Broker

- Not all brokers are equal. So, how do business owners confirm that they are getting the best program available, without going through a broker bidding war?

There are a few ways that people purchase insurance today. One way is to shop via the internet. The internet is an incredible tool for gaining access to information.

- Do you think the level of trust is higher or lower when dealing strictly via the internet?

Just because I can file my taxes on-line, doesn't mean I still don't hire a professional accountant. The premiums offered on the internet may be slightly lower than when using a broker. However, the level of trust gained when dealing with a trained professional, is always greater.

A second way people purchase insurance coverage is to employ "Broker Warfare." That's where multiple brokers go out and "shop" the insurance marketplace. The hope is that the broker with the lowest bid will win the business. News flash! Hope is not a strategy! When buyers of insurance intend to send multiple brokers into the marketplace on a marketing competition they are making a huge mistake. In fact, chances are they will end up paying more for their coverage and possibly could put the stability of their insurance program in jeopardy. There are multiple reasons for that.

1. Limited Marketplace - In today's market, there are a limited number of carriers willing to compete and that have an appetite for a particular type of risk. Years ago we marketed our way out of price increases. We brokers had a long list of carriers that no longer exist today (Home, Reliance, Aetna, Kemper, Royal & Sun Alliance, AIG, Mission, Maryland Casualty, Continental, St. Paul, etc. etc.). These insurers all competed against each other ferociously. We would tell the

underwriters, "Get to this price, we will deliver the deal!" Buyers loved the falling prices but in the end all it did was eliminate carriers.

2. Muddied Field - Most reputable brokers all represent the same carriers. A business needs their story told by one strong consistent voice. The worst thing that can happen is that an underwriter will receive multiple submissions, from different brokers and the submissions don't match. That always translates into higher costs for the insured, or worse yet, a possible "NO". This has the potential of eliminating a viable insurer from an already limited field. Don't forget, underwriters love to practice quote ☺

3. Broker Skill - The ability to market a client's program must be done in a very precise manner. Marketplace allocation does not account for the different skill levels and relationships of the broker. It's based solely on who is assigned markets or sometimes who can run a photocopier the fastest. Clients may get the right insurance company for their coverage but might not necessarily get the best broker to manage the relationship.

I once received a call from a prospect (now a client) that was with one of the big brokerage houses. They had their policy cancel and could not get a reinstatement. I called an underwriter and she told me, "Paul, this account is ugly, it has high losses and was just lapsed for non-pay, but because you're on it, we'll give it a shot." Markets are cyclical in nature and they rise and fall all the time. The old fashioned marketplace competition just doesn't work anymore, that's why relationships are more important.

Another option for purchasing insurance involves the "request for proposal," approach. The "RFP," is what we commonly refer to as the "Beauty Contest." Business owners will screen and evaluate multiple brokers based on their capabilities to reduce the overall costs. The broker that's selected is granted access to all the carriers based on demonstrated abilities that work towards reducing the client's total cost of risk. What a concept.　Aren't expertise and proficiency implied when you open for business and target accounts?　I think it used to be called competency.

Winning brokers need to shift their thinking.　We are not solely insurance sales people, we're consultants that help clients reduce costs by being gatekeepers of resources.　There are many strategies that lower insurance costs.　Yet, the real key is developing relationships that add value to a clients business.　I understand the RFP is a necessity when dealing with certain types of entities (municipalities, governments, large non-profits, etc.).　In my experience, the RFP is 99.9% political.　There is always a leader on any board.　There's the one individual that is guiding the process and who exerts more influence than the others.　That is the person that needs to be courted.　Identify and build a relationship with that person and your chances of winning are exponentially increased.

I entered a board room surrounded by the CEO and all the other members of the board.　I had only been allowed the meeting due to the relationship I had established with a banker friend of mine that had a strong relationship with the CEO.　My target was to win only two pieces of the insurance program (Workers Compensation & D&O).　I presented all my supporting data and proof of expertise in those two areas addressing the CEO directly.　At the end of the meeting he turned to the board and made the decision to hire us on the spot.　No RFP necessary, no debate.　By not being greedy and only tackling two (very lucrative) pieces of their program (incidentally we improved coverage and saved them costs), we won a great deal.　I leveraged my friendship with a key influencer in order to get my foot in the door with the decision maker.　No one said this was going to be easy but with the right amount of determination (and a modicum of competency) it can be done.

There have been many instances where winning a small portion of the client's insurance program (portions where you have extreme competency) is the smartest strategy.　For additional strategies to winning large accounts with TCOR principles, try visiting C.R. "Rob" Ekern @ Consultative Brokerage: A Value Strategy.

"A friendship founded on business is better than a business founded on friendship."
John D. Rockefeller

"The most dangerous poison is the feeling of achievement. The antidote is to every evening think what can be done better tomorrow."
Ingvar Kamprad, IKEA founder

Chapter 9

How to add Value

Adding value is like trying to define the ultimate widget. What is it really? In my search, the best explanation I've read comes from Jeffery Gittomer, in his book, <u>The little Red Sales Book of Selling</u>. After completing a survey of over 10,000 business owners he compiled the following list of what every business owner wants:

1. More Sales
2. More Profit
3. More free time
4. More customers
5. Better Image
6. Better Morale
7. Notoriety
8. No Hassles
9. Greater Productivity
10. Loyal Employees

It's our job to affect these areas of our client's businesses. ***This is called adding value!*** We should be looking out constantly for opportunities not only to improve their bottom line but also to solve their dilemmas. We become an extension of our clients business when we add value for them. When I started my sales system strategy, I wanted to focus on two things.

1. Identify the common concerns in my industry and figure out best practices to resolving those concerns.

2. What can I do to bring value to the prospect first?

Lower premiums and cutting costs are good. Every client expects their agent to access multiple markets, service the account and negotiate the best prices, terms and conditions of their insurance contracts. In reality, this is the bare minimum of service expectations. Time for a reality check, price is rarely the main objection to a sale. Clients will pay a fair price (not necessarily the cheapest) if you bring them value. <u>Transactions</u> are rarely value driven based, whereas <u>value</u> and <u>relationships</u> can overcome price all day long. By seeking to improve your client's business you move from vendor status to *trusted* advisor (there's that "trust" word again).

- How much would you have to worry about losing to a competitor if your services created better employee morale, increased employee productivity or decreased employee turnover?

- What do you think the odds are of losing a client to a lower price, if you've already driven millions of dollars in referral business to that client?

If you said, "not much," you're right! Partner relationships are some of the strongest bonds that are made. They are rarely broken, therefore, the importance of maintaining them can't be emphasized enough. Make it easy to do business with you versus your competitor.

On one occasion one of my clients had just lost a key employee to a competitor. I asked them who they had in line for succession. They were not prepared for the event and did not have anyone with the specific skill set to fill the position. I knew what they were looking for and, with their permission, I confidentially called a few of my other clients for some advice. One of them had just been through a similar interview process and knew an excellent candidate that was runner-up in their search. I asked if I could contact him and they provided me with his information. I forwarded it to my client, they got in contact with him and two weeks later he was hired. My client was so grateful that I could help them. They had no down time and the transition was seamless. Do you think their loyalty to me will be changed when another broker comes in to bid and quote their insurance program? Helping others by providing value is the best security.

"It is rare to find a business partner who is selfless. If you are lucky it happens once in a lifetime."
Michael Eisner

Chapter 10
The Value Driven Culture

During an introductory meeting a business man was asked, "What makes your company better than your closest competitors? It's probably your employees, right? The business owner said, absolutely not, my competitor can take my best employees tomorrow, but he can never, ever, steal my CULTURE." What a wake-up call, and he was right. Your company's culture is driven from the top down. Ownership and upper management drive the culture of every organization. The culture of an organization speaks volumes about trust, commitment, results and opportunity.

<u>How Healthy is Your Corporate Culture?</u>

- Does your company embrace acceptance and appreciation for diversity? How?
- Is your culture creative, imaginative, vibrant, fun and growing? Or is it a staunch, dry, quiet, reserved and just get the job done culture?
- Is it a culture of "yes," let's see how to accomplish that? Or is it a culture of, "sorry" we can't accommodate that request / it's never been done like that before?
- Is there strong communication with all employees regarding policies and company issues? Or does upper management have the "Ivory Tower Syndrome" (Where executives rarely leave their offices to communicate, inspire or encourage the employees)?
- Does your CEO and upper management persuade and lead by instilling confidence with an open door policy and frequent team meetings? Or are corporate goals and objectives communicated mostly through email or the "chain of command?"
- What's the one question you hope you hope buyers never ask?
- Is there a high regard for and fair treatment of each employee as well as respect for each employee's contribution to the company?
- Is there employee pride and enthusiasm for the organization and the work?

- If there were an anonymous idea and suggestion survey done, how would your colleagues describe the atmosphere of the company?
- How does your company make a point to personally welcome new hires?
- Is there equal opportunity for each employee to realize their full potential within the company?
- Is there incentive and investment in learning, training, and employee knowledge?
- What do your competitors fear most about your company?
- What was your most recent customer defection and why did it happen?
- What improvements would you make if you had the budget and the resources?
- Which type of environment do you think has better morale, lower turnover, lower mistakes and higher profits?
- Which type of culture would you rather work for?

Every organization, a church, a school, a government, or a company has a culture. And every company has strengths and weaknesses that fit the profile of their industry. Performance oriented cultures statistically have better financial growth than others. Those corporate cultures have high levels of communication with employees and encourage healthy risk taking. Emphasis on accountability and employee education typically experience higher performance and profitability as well.

I have worked for many types of organizations and experienced very different cultures. One of the best organizations I worked for had a culture that was absolutely contagious. I actually said, TGIM, "Thank God It's Monday." Once per month, the company would cater a luncheon with really great food. Every employee was in attendance. There were also guests that were invited to this luncheon that consisted of clients, prospects and vendor suppliers. Each department within the company was given one month to determine the theme of the lunch and perform the set up and decoration. For instance, during March there was typically an Irish theme to coincide with St. Patrick's Day celebrations. The tables all had green clover table clothes, a center piece, cups of green M&M's and green glitter.

A typical luncheon lasted about an hour and a half and included the following agenda.

✓ Great catered food - Lunch served to all employees and guests.
✓ All new business won or retained during the previous month read aloud.
✓ All employee birthdays and anniversaries (tenure with company) read aloud and presented with a card of appreciation. Personal information was read aloud about the person (ex: She has two dogs, loves to fish, married with a grandchild on the way, etc..) whereby the employees would guess the employee being talked about.
✓ All "Raving Fan" awards read aloud - Raving Fan's are notes passed on by clients about the exceptional service of an employee. Mystery money envelopes for Raving Fan picks were also doled out.
✓ All guests were introduced and invited to share a quick 30 second commercial about their company. Guests included vendors, new clients and prospects.
✓ A quick fun game or piece of trivia was played and the winners took home the center pieces
✓ A warm thank you from the CEO was always included and ended the event.

Recognition for talent, a job well done and gratitude towards our clients and potential clients was emphasized. It was exciting, professional, enthusiastic, fun and filled with encouragement. The company experienced unprecedented growth, loyalty was developed and an appreciative culture was enforced. Does that sound like a company you would like to have been part of? Is that what you have now (perhaps yours is even better!)?

When people meet you and the other employees of your company, they form an impression of the culture within. That "brand" is not just the appearance of the offices or the clothes that the employees are allowed to wear. The brand is the stamp people place upon you and your company. It encompasses your reputation for reliability, trust, competence and professionalism. Essentially, *you* are the brand of the company. People will form an impression of your company the moment they meet *you*.

- If you had to guess, what do you think people are saying about your culture?
- Do you have a platform for being notified about what customers and team members think about the culture (suggestion box, direct email to the CEO etc.)?
- What actions are you taking to improve the brand of the company?

There's an old saying in Christianity that says, "If you find the perfect church, don't join it, because you'll only ruin it." Groucho Marx said, "I would never join a club that would accept me as a member." Like churches and clubs, there are no perfect companies. Even if they did exist, we would probably ruin them if we joined them. Thankfully, there are some amazing company cultures. Don't like your situation, change yourself. Still not working, change your company. Not satisfied still? Create your own. Life's too short to settle on miserable. Finding the right culture or creating the right one is where people thrive and grow.

"I have found no greater satisfaction than achieving success through honest dealing and strict adherence to the view that, for you to gain, those you deal with should gain as well."
Alan Greenspan

"Wise men once said that a person is known by the company he keeps. It can also be said that a company is known by the people it keeps."
Stan Slap

Chapter 11
Building a Winning Team

I will never forget watching the USA amateur hockey team beat the professionals of the Soviet Union in the 1980 Olympics. It was the <u>Miracle on Ice</u> and the pinnacle of team work. Coach Herb Brooks was known for his hard abrasive style yet he allowed Captain Mike Eruzione to inspire his fellow teammates. With the mantra, "Play your game, play your game!" the Americans never let up and shocked the USSR and the world. Likewise, the company that breeds success is served and empowered by the leadership above. Yes, there will be hard leaders to please, but if the vision is clear and the goals are high, hard work can lead to amazing things. Winning companies are meritocracies that reward and recognize achievement from the least to the greatest. They respect candor from their associates, not malevolent dishonesty. They expect initiative and guts from the sales force in the organization. They know that the sales force is only as good as their team's ability to deliver on the services and product expected by the client.

I told my wife years ago that we were a team, but I was the captain. And like most women, she lets me believe that for as long as she likes. There are many qualities to a winning sales team. As a rule, you have front line sales leaders that drive the relationship, tell the jokes, wine, dine and make the high commissions. Then the rest of the team does all the work (unfortunately, some think this isn't a joke!). The advantage of great teams is their leader's ability to manage the process and lead the team towards the end goal. Former President Dwight D. Eisenhower used to illustrate the art of leadership in much the same way. He'd place a piece of string on a table and say, "Pull it and it will follow you anywhere you wish. Push it and it will go nowhere at all." Successful sales people are often leaders in most organizations because sales people and leaders share at least two common traits.

1. Leaders share the same ability to handle rejection well. They have convictions towards a cause and exhibit confidence.

2. Leaders are calculated risk takers. Typically they are not afraid to leave the comfort that comes with the status quo. They view risk as a fuel for growth.

A well oiled sales team is one in which all members know their roles and each one performs their part of the mission. Good leaders surround themselves with great support. That's the success behind the Walt Disney Corporation, where every employee is a "cast member," understanding their specific assignments and roles. Each one supports the vision of the organization as a whole.

- Do you know your role?
- Will that role be expanded or contracted?
- How much of that do you think depends on you?

I used to tell my children that when they entered a new school or found themselves on a new sports team (where they did not know the other children), not to worry about finding friends. It was more important to be the right person than to find the right person. Therefore, being a good teammate is much more important than finding good team mates. The essence of being a good team mate rests in a willingness to serve. One does not need to be a doormat in order to serve. There is an ancient Chinese proverb that offers profound insight on this. The story is told that,

"The reason why rivers and seas receive homage of a hundred mountain streams is that they keep below them. Thus they are able to reign over all mountain streams. So the sage wishing to be above men will put himself below them, wishing to be before them he puts himself behind them. Though his place be above men, they do not feel his weight, though his place be before them, they do not count it an injury" So it is with mankind, those who wish to yield the greatest influence will unselfishly position themselves below others so as to serve them better."

Working to accomplish the goals of the company, assisting colleagues and creating satisfied customers, fosters winning teams. In his book Winning,

Jack Welch states that corporate values are really corporate behaviors. Those behaviors fall into ten basic categories.

1. Never let profit center conflicts get in the way of doing what's best for the customer.
2. Give a fair deal.
3. Always look for ways to make it easier to do business with you.
4. Don't forget to personally say thank you.
5. Communicate regularly with your customers, if they're talking to you they can't be talking to the competition.
6. Eliminate bureaucracy make it easy to say yes.
7. Value each other's time.
8. Cut waste relentlessly.
9. Operations should be fast and simple.
10. Reward the people who exhibit the core values and punish those who don't.

- What are your corporate values and how do they mesh with your actions and attitude?

There is great synergy when behaviors that your company values above others, match your own. Since culture changes with leadership, strive to lead where you are. It's this type of altruism that will drive a culture of growth and success. John Ilhan said, *"If you treat staff as your equal, they'll roll their sleeves up to get the job done."*

Teams don't have to revolve around one specific sales person and their support staff. In fact, an interesting trend in some of the most successful sales organizations today involves the team sales approach. Team selling involves splitting profits by pairing up two producers and their account teams. It can be a delicate balance that takes the right chemistry but, like a great marriage, it can prove to be a strong and creative atmosphere. A salesperson with specific strengths might do well with another salesperson that has those weaknesses (albeit with complementary strengths). In some instances, a seasoned professional will mentor a newer sales person and exponentially boost the learning curve. This approach might not work in every organization but it has worked miracles for others.

In many instances there are sales teams where two competing sales people have a different internal relationship with the same prospect. In one instance I knew the CFO and my colleague knew the CEO. Our manager brought us into his office and asked us to give him our most compelling argument as to who should work the account. I said, "If Bill has the better relationship with the CEO then, by all means, I want him to take the account." Bill immediately said, "If Paul knows the CFO, he should take the account." We smiled at each other and ended up becoming sales team partners tackling and splitting the account together." By both of us being unselfish, we discovered each other's character. Through compromise, and a willingness to achieve the end goal, each of us won.

There's so much more to be said on mature leadership and its importance to team building. For excellent core concepts on empowered organizations and leadership, I recommend materials from Ken Blanchard, Dr. Stephen Covey and Dr. John Maxwell. Lead by example, perform with excellence and be prepared for contingencies.

"Being powerful is like being a lady. If you have to tell people you are, then you're not."
Margaret Thatcher

"Teamwork makes the dream work, but a vision becomes a nightmare when the leader has a big dream and a bad team."
John C. Maxwell

Chapter 12
Introductions and First Meetings.

When we talk about introductions there are a few common types that come to mind.

1. How presentable are you when meeting for the first time.
2. What's the agenda at an "introductory first meeting?"
3. Who are you and what do you do (Elevator speeches)?

<u>First Impressions</u>

A. My dad told me that first impressions, just like appearances, are invaluable, so make sure yours is a good one. He didn't always follow his own advice, especially when I went through his tie rack. But the point is clear. Dressing the part of a professional is the first step. It depends on what you are selling and to whom. Most likely you wouldn't wear a suit and tie to market the latest rodeo gear. <u>Common sense is the rule.</u> It's always easier to dress a little more formal for a meeting and be able to tone it down by removing a jacket than it is to show up in a polo shirt and put on a tie. For most salesmen, a new introduction to a prospect is one of the most exciting moments in sales. It sets the whole tone of the conversation and the expectations of each party. Every first call starts with a plan and an agenda. Dress and speak the part of a professional.

B. Impressions are formed through our communication skills. We communicate with appearance, tone of voice, inflection, pace of speech, the words we use and with body language. Those that play poker know what a "tell" is. A "tell" is, the subtle but detectable change in a player's behavior or demeanor that gives clues to that player's assessment of his hand. A key to communicating friendship comes from a simple little tell. It's the most universally recognized communication devices that we all have, it is (drum roll please)..... "The smile." We can discuss the importance of posture, the proper handshake and etiquette but nothing is more universally acknowledged than, the smile. When was the last time you checked your smile?

C. Some sales people speak in technical terminology that may **only** be familiar to experts within their field. Remember the story of the Texas consultant that's called over to Germany for some work (see chapter on Listening pg. 29). Keep your jargon at home unless you're sure your audience knows exactly what you mean.

We need to make sure we are speaking the same language as the prospect. Speak their language and stay away from industry jargon that may be unfamiliar to your prospect. First impressions are priceless and it's difficult to get a second chance, therefore, plain speak is gooderer speak (yes I realize it should probably be besterer).

"Good people never think they've reached the top of their game but they're dying to get there."
Jack Welch

Two Great Ways to Start a Meeting

There are many great ways to start a consultative meeting. David Sandler (Sandler Sales Training) popularized the NOT method. It follows an acronym that stands for Naturally, Obviously, and Typically. The conversation flows naturally, is very non-confrontational and the format confirms next steps with an up-front contract (UFC). It sounds something like this:

NOT (Naturally, Obviously, Typically)

Naturally Mrs. _____ you'll have some questions about (my organization), our background, our services and examples of some of the phenomenal results experienced by our clients. **Obviously**, I want to confirm what I already know about your company, your culture, vision and objectives. **Typically**, at the end of our conversation we can discuss potential next steps. I'm OK if there isn't a fit, if you are comfortable telling me so. Is that fair? The topics I hear most people have concerns with include what people are trying to fix accomplish or avoid inside "PARC." What subjects are you most concerned with?

Another great way to start a meeting is to provide an introductory lead in and then let the prospect take over.

PLMH (Please Let Me Help)

Mr. _____ similar to any good attorney or doctor, as an insurance professional I would never present solutions to a problem until I first understood what your problems are. Any broker can quote your insurance program and they typically look to do that around your expiration dates of your policies. The reason expirations dates of your policies is not so important is because problems, issues and solutions don't revolve around expiration dates. Generally when we're talking to businesses about their insurance program they describe similar problems concerning (see PARC chapter). I'd like to touch on some of those issues and focus on strategies that can reduce your costs and increase your profitability.

- Can we talk about what you're trying to fix, accomplish or avoid?
- Where would you like to start?

Great introductions set the atmosphere of the whole sales call. The sales person that is honestly trying to figure out the prospects agenda before pursuing their own earns much more respect. Be honest with your prospect and let them know that your agenda is not to sell them anything. On the contrary, your main objective in the introductory meeting is to determine if there's a good business fit between what you offer and what they need.

"Give people enough guidance to make the decisions you want them to make. Don't tell them what to do, but encourage them to do what is best."
Jimmy Johnson

Chapter 13

X-Dates

There are some that say X-Date follow up is essential and others that will say it is unimportant. Let's settle the argument once and for all. In the beginning of the book (Introduction to Lessons Learned) I spoke about the difference between large and small sales. Most property and casualty (P&C) insurance contracts lock in a rate for either six or twelve months. Those that sell personal lines (auto, homeowners, boat, motorcycle etc.) typically are dealing with smaller premiums and X-Dates become more important to refer to and utilize. Generally in commercial P&C (business insurance) there are smaller sales (premiums under $15K) middle market (premiums up to $350K) and large sales. X-Dates are important for smaller sales and some middle market. However, middle market and most large sales typically have PARC issues that can be resolved irrespective of the expiration of the policies. That's when forming a relationship trumps transaction costs and x-dates. Benefits insurance sales (health, dental, vision etc.) also work with both individuals and groups (businesses). For many benefits opportunities, the X-Date is typically irrelevant if there is a better program available. The rationale is that the change can be made on a month to month basis rather than waiting for the annual renewal.

If the reasons for changing a policy are compelling enough for the client (Probe the PARC System) then the expiration of a policy becomes irrelevant. Use common sense. If, after you've done your due diligence, it makes sense to take an agent of record letter on a client immediately (so you can correct their PARC issues/errors) then justify your case with the client. Just make sure you don't become an unpaid consultant (providing answers, solutions and strategies on how to resolve their issues) without their commitment to you. People will do business with who they want, when they want, based on their reasons, not ours.

Their #1 value is ethics. Their # 2 is responding to customers and their #3 is profits. They're saying, "We won't do anything that will improve our profit if it is unethical or responsive to customers."
Ken Blanchard

Chapter 14

Do Prospects Lie?

Has this ever happened to you? You are well into a sales cycle, qualified the prospect, established rapport and identified all the areas you know you can resolve with your services. The prospect has provided you with all their information so that you can quote their insurance program. This can be a large commitment on your part with the possibility of not obtaining a sale. You have gathered the following minimum information:

- Previous policies for all lines of coverage including all terms/conditions and exclusions
- Confirmed current values of all property, age, construction and updates to all buildings,
- Drivers and vehicle information, schedules, areas and scope of operation, type of cargo
- Current issues, concerns or potential risks for decision makers (any mergers or acquisition plans, deductible or co-insurance issues etc.)
- Previous three - five years claims experience (loss runs) on all lines of coverage
- Competition - who else is working on the account, what carriers were approached and when

After significant time and resources you've determined which carriers have an appetite for the business, you've schedule loss control surveys, and negotiated the best terms and conditions from the carriers. Finally you and your team develop and rehearse your presentation. You then deliver your proposals in a professional manner and the prospect tells you,

- ➢ "I need to think about it."
- ➢ "I'll need to pass this by management or the board before a final decision is made."
- ➢ "Your firm did an excellent job and you are definitely in the running, we will get back with you shortly."

➢ "We are eager to make a decision and will call you back in a couple of days."

A few days later, you're waiting for the prospect's call... and the phone is not ringing. These are all lies, you've just been used and have become the dreaded, "unpaid consultant." No amount of follow up calls will land you the deal. "All Cretans are liars shouted the Cretan!" The contradiction of the statement is obvious, is he lying or isn't he? The funny thing is, most sales people think too many prospects are Cretans. Why do they do this and more importantly, how do you avoid this? Sometimes the prospect used your information for knowledge. Other times they just used your information to renegotiate with their current vendor (keep them honest). Prospects aren't sadistic or stupid. Many don't want to hurt the feelings of the sales person and this is their way of avoiding confrontation and criticism. So, "What do I do when the prospect is reluctant to answer truthfully due to the lack of rapport or business trust?" First, you should re-state your commitment as a consultant looking to see if there is a business fit (Introductions pg.101). Then, say, "Sometimes people are uncomfortable answering my questions honestly because they don't want to hurt my feeling or they have another agent that they are working with, (I get the feeling) or is that the case here?" On rare occasions, the sales person did not properly identify the decision maker with the true power. Shame on them! Like mom always said, "honesty is the best policy."

"O, what a tangled web we weave, when first we practice to deceive!"
Sir Walter Scott

How to avoid the preceding scenario from repeating itself

The keys to winning the sale and developing a relationship include:

1. Identify their PARC concerns.
1. Confirm what's going to happen (expectations) at the conclusion of your presentation.

Before you provide solutions and undergo all the work, ask the prospect:

Mr. Prospect, suppose I were to find the best carrier that has an appetite for your business, conduct all the loss control surveys, negotiate the best terms and conditions you're looking for, package all the information in a proposal and make a presentation where we thoroughly demonstrated how we would do precisely what you require, which is to resolve your concerns with (re-state their main PARC Method concerns). What would happen then?"

In an instant, you've done all the work. Paint the picture of a perfect scenario and determine if you like how they tell the ending. If the prospect is not willing to make a commitment to an action that is in your best interest (sitting by the phone for days waiting for a decision is definitely not in your best interest) you probably shouldn't commit to doing the work. Continuously confirming next steps is pivotal to not wasting you, your team or your prospects time. There is no, "what's going to happen next," in professional sales.

If you believe you must follow the process of committing time and resources (after all, underwriters love practice quoting), then charge a fee for your work. Agree to apply the fee against commissions or your service fee if you earn the business. This strategy won't guarantee you'll get the sale, but at the very least, you'll get paid for your efforts and avoid becoming an **unpaid** consultant. I know what you're thinking; all the other brokers aren't charging a fee to quote. Re-read Choosing a Broker (pg. 82) and decide how you want to educate your prospect in obtaining the best deal on their insurance program.

If you can't come to an agreement, sometimes it's best to walk away (sometimes it just isn't a good fit). It's easy to say and harder to do but don't become too emotionally attached to making a sale. Stick with your plan to find and qualify the most profitable type of clients. In the long run you will have higher retention, develop stronger relationships and experience more frequent referrals.

"Fool me once shame on you, fool me twice shame on me."
Scotty Chief engineer of the U.S.S. Enterprise (Star Trek)

Chapter 15
What's Your Main Differentiator?

This question drove me crazy for years, let's settle this. Sales people are on the front line of the company every day. They are the ones that directly come up against the competitions offerings every day. It's been said that, imitation is the sincerest art of flattery. In the business world there is never anything that is proprietary for long. If there's profit to be made, competitors will always try to match your technology, accessibility, programs and prices (rates). If everyone is copying each other, than what makes a firm truly different?

- What do your competitors fear most about your product, your company and you?
- How do competitors try to differentiate themselves from you?
- What do your competitors claim to buyers is the major weakness of your company and you?
- What's the one question you hope buyers never ask?
- Why do your best customers continue to do business with you (what do they like best), and are you sure about the answer?
- Where was your most recent customer defection and why did it happen?
- In your opinion, what is the number one improvement you would you make (if you had the budget and resources) to increase market share?
- What are your biggest obstacles that need to be overcome (reliability, delivery, prestige, service, tech support)?

I use to send literature with the following information showing why I thought my firm was unique.

Ten Things to Consider Before Selecting a Broker

1. Ease of doing business and Practice Groups - we thoroughly understand manufacturer and distributor's risk
2. Accessibility - each client is assigned a dedicated support team and risk manager to the account available 24/7

3.   Commitment to innovation – alternative program options, risk management strategies, Technology, and assistance in loss controls
4.   Local, National and International capabilities
5.   Reputation of our firm and marketplace leverage – access to most "A" rated carriers and premium volume to negotiate the most favorable rates and terms of coverage for our clients
6.   Customer Service Contract - supports pro-active services. Lists which initiatives we will work on, responsible parties and completion deadlines
7.   Marketing Summaries – shows detailed carrier appetite, underwriter notes, and negotiated terms keeping us accountable to our clients
8.   On Staff - Claims adjusters, Third Party Administrator (TPA), analytics services and auditor services working for you not the carriers.
9.   Workers Compensation mod verification, feasibility study, program analysis and claims mitigation
10. Stewardship reports – unsurpassed communication of all activities are documented for your review

We offer all these additional Value Added Services in house, to our clients, at NO additional cost.

Blah, Blah, Blah, Blah, Blah! Big whoopdeedoo. If I had bothered to do my research, I would have found almost all my major competitors stating the very same thing. The second kicker I received was from my manager. I actually had management tell me once that the main differentiator was the corporation's size and branding. With a popular and well known name we were to, "Sell the Enterprise." I kept thinking, sorry, I am not Captain Kirk. Here's a revelation, the main differentiator to every sale is…. YOU! Take a look in the mirror, that's right, YOU. You are the face of the product and service for the company. When a sale is made, 99.9% of the time the client didn't buy the price, the product or the company, they bought you. The client put their trust in you. You were the difference, in the approach, the follow up and the delivery. When I realized that the main difference for the company I worked for was me, it gave me confidence that I could succeed anywhere, and confidence is a huge advantage in sales.

"Fake it til you make it" (also called "act as if"). It means that imitating confidence and success will generate real confidence. The goal is to avoid getting stuck in a *self fulfilling prophecy* related to one's fear of not being confident. Confidence has a strangely deep connection with the attitude of gratitude. Until you like and accept yourself right where you are, you will not enjoy life nor its journey, and to the extent you accept and like YOU, determines how effectively you can share confidence with others both personally and professionally. You can't fake being grateful. To be clear, we should be confident based on vision, facts, goals and mission. I'm not talking about being sincere. I have met some very sincere people before, unfortunately, some have been sincerely wrong.

In sales, the uncertainty aspects typically revolve around the details and minutia. We all know the devil is in the details, so, confirm your answers. Learn as much about your company's services and procedures as possible. It's OK to not know something. If you don't know, volunteer to get back with an answer, just make sure you get it right before you communicate it. When you always tell the truth you never have to remember what you said. A career in sales requires confidence. Confidence is based in trust and truth. Certainty that your team or your service will deliver the stated value to a prospect is confidence. Be confident, you are the difference!

"When people believe in themselves they have the first secret of success."
Norman Vincent Peale

"To succeed in life you need two things; Ignorance and Confidence."
Mark Twain

"Confidence comes not from always being right but from not fearing to be wrong."
Peter T McIntyre

Chapter 16
The Elevator Speech (30 Second Commercials)

- When someone asks, "What do you do for a living," how do you respond?

If you're like most people, you tell them your title and the name of the company that you work for. Unfortunately, in most cases, this does nothing to stimulate interest on behalf of the listener. That's where the 30 second commercial or "elevator pitch" comes into play. The name "elevator pitch" reflects the idea that your speech should be possible to deliver in about the time it takes to ride up an elevator (between 30 seconds to 1 minute).

Wouldn't it be better to preface your answer to "What do you do?" with a question or statement that focuses on the problem your product or service addresses? An elevator speech is a well practiced concise overview and brief description of the benefits of your company's products and services. Most elevator pitches answer some pivotal questions.

1. What is your product or service (described briefly without going into detail)?
2. Who is your target market?
3. What's your competitive advantage?
4. What are the benefits or typical results experienced by those who use your product or service (what's in it for them)?
5. Call for action - what would you like them to do after they hear it.

Good elevator speeches contain a hook or statement that gets the listeners attention. This can be phrased as a typical problem experienced by those that you help. If the pitch is going to last about 30 seconds, that equates to approximately 50 - 75 words.

- ➤ Generic: Have you ever had to deal with a customer service representative for a company you do business with and it seems as if YOUR sense of urgency is never THEIR sense of urgency?

Well I help resolve that in the area of insurance. I work with Donovan Insurance Solutions and we believe our client's needs need to be resolved quickly, correctly and personally. Our professionalism, and transparency help build the trust that keep us accountable to our customers.

or

> You know how some CEO's and business owners have headaches with their insurance program? They experience skyrocketing premiums, receive their renewals at the last minute, have severe or frequent claims issues or even simply have a hard time getting a hold of their broker for service. My name is Paul Donovan and I'm an insurance and risk management consultant. I resolve thosee aggravating issues with insurance programs. Besides premium savings, the mental freedom from worry is typically the focus. If it makes sense and I can help you or someone you know, I would be happy to share some strategies when it's convenient. How about you, what do you do?

Introduce "needs" with other phrases such as, "Do you know how...," "You probably haven't thought about...," or "Would you be surprised to find out..."

> Would you be surprised to find out that typically the highest expense for businesses after payroll and taxes revolves around a company's insurance program? As a risk management consultant I help companies resolve their major insurance issues that could include: premium increases, accountability, renewal processes, adding strategic resources, claims mitigation, and coverage options. I've never had so much fun helping businesses lower costs. If it makes sense and you know someone that could use my services, here's my card. How about you, what do you do?

To get your prospects' attention and arouse their curiosity, first focus on their challenges (The PARC Method), then introduce your solution. The most pivotal part of the pitch has to be in the delivery. It should sound natural, sincere, not "canned" and you should know it by heart. To really take it to the next level, have 2-3 variations of your speech available in your repertoire to fit the audience you're engaged with. Preparation is the key. Do your homework first. If you want great answers to a common question, prepare the answer beforehand. You must write it out, cut out the techno-jargon and be real, after that, it's the same way you get to Carnegie Hall, practice practice, practice.

"My job is to talk to you, and your job is to listen. If you finish first, please let me know."
Harry Hershfield

Chapter 17
Closing Techniques?

In one of the most famous sales movies of all time, Glengarry Glen Ross, Alec Baldwin's character tells his sales people to ABC, Always Be Closing. That is the stereotypical personification of the "cheesy sales guy." There's something about the term "closing" that harkens back to the old carnival barker on the midway, not the professional. Early in my career, my manager trained everyone on all the closing techniques that were staples in the salesman's repertoire. Closing techniques that we learned included:

1. *Assumptive close* – where would you like it delivered (before the customer has agreed to buy).

2. *Last Chance/Deal is off Close* – The price goes up next week unless you buy now.

3. *Alternative Close* – Would you prefer delivery on Tuesday or Thursday.

4. *Standing Room Only Close* – If you can't make a decision right now I'll have to offer it to another customer who's pressing to buy.

5. *Blank Order Close* – Where one fills in the customers answers on an order form even though the buyer hasn't indicated a willingness to purchase yet.

6. *My Pen or Yours* - Would you rather use my pen or yours to sign the contract?

7. *Ben Franklin Close* - where you draw a T, and on one side you list all of the disadvantages of the purchase and on the other you list the advantages. The side with the most items wins the decision.

8. *Convenience Close* - Internet shopping, instant emails/texts, fast food windows one stop shopping - Accessibility 24/7 is the

convenience factor. Testimonials are used to prove your case.

9. *The String of Yes's Close* - where the salesman gets the prospect agreeing on one subject after another stringing together multiple yes answers to questions and then asking for the order in that freight car of reasoning.

- How do you feel about these hard closing techniques?
- Does it make you feel more professional or less?
- When people use these techniques on you, are you more or less inclined to purchase?

These tired, worn out, old fashioned ways of getting business were supposed to make the sale. When these types of closing techniques are used to produce a sale, I found two things inevitably happened.

1. The likelihood of buyer's remorse is always increased.
2. Business retention goes down.

People don't want to purchase under pressure and that's all closing techniques really are. They pressure the prospect into a decision to purchase that is based on the sales persons reasons not the prospects. Interest is always measured in actions not words and it always involves commitment.

The consultative approach asks the prospect the best way to proceed?

- What's the next step or what do you think we should do next?
- What would you like me to do or what do you think we should do next?
- What's the best way I can help?
- Does it make sense to start the process?
- Looks like we're on the same page, do you have any questions before we move forward?

The United States Marine Corps have a great billboard recruiting poster that reads, "We don't take applications just commitments." Meaning, they don't recruit soldiers, they develop them. The implication is, that with a commitment toward training, people can be built up, molded, and grow into their chosen career path. If I were creating a billboard for successful salespeople it would say, "We don't deal in transactions, we build relationships." In sales, transactions are typically short-term one shot deals, whereas relationships provide multiple long-term deals. Relational sales typically have higher premiums involved and are more profitable. Every sales person knows that it's easier to sell and keep an existing client and harder to create new ones. Therefore, it makes sense to build relationships on trust that can generate multiple sales over time.

Handling Objections the Easy Way?

The risk of making any purchase could include:

> Financial risk
> Is there a need for it
> May be able to get it for less money
> It is not what was envisioned/perceived or thought at first
> Service after sale won't be there
> Something better exists (impossible to buy electronics today with this mindset)
> Priorities are different
> Don't trust the sales person

Risk is actually a lack of confidence, trust, believability, service, company or in one's self. This causes doubt and doubts result in objections. The four most common objections that people have, boil down to: price, competition, will it work and timing (not now). The traditional methods for overcoming them include:

1. Feel, Felt, Found technique - I can understand how you **feel**, many of my best customers have also **felt** that way. However, when they gave me a moment to explain, they readily **found** that they received the lowest total cost of ownership......

2. Present an Alternative - That's one way to look at the situation. However, another way to look at it is (here comes your alternative) if you consider the potential impact of…. On your business, you would see you would receive a much greater value with our solution. For example, we recently helped …..

You're thinking OK then, what's **the easiest ways to handle objections**

Objection prevention is more important than *objection handling*. Before your prospect can raise a common objection it is easier to bring up the objection before the prospect does. You can then preemptively present solutions that diffuse the angst. Once you've identified their primary PARC concern(s), you must then offer a proof statement. Relay a true story of a strategy that helped resolve a prospect with a similar concern. True examples of success help ease the prospects anxiety over your credibility. If you don't have your own experience to draw on for examples, ask a colleague, manager or seasoned professional about how an issue was resolved by the company.

If there is no relationship the trustworthiness of the salesperson is very low. Therefore, credibility needs to be established. There are a few great ways to establish credibility.

A trusted friend that provides a reference is invaluable to overcoming trust issues. Letter references are OK, video is better but the best referral is a warm handshake to handshake, in person, introduction. Nothing screams trust like a personal face to face endorsement. To get referrals like this, make referrals like this. We spoke briefly about altruism in the PALACES chapter under <u>Endurance and Encouragement</u>.

Transparency also speaks volumes to the unfamiliar prospect. In your opinion, how many people that buy insurance have ever been asked, "What did you pay your broker?" Isn't that a fair question? *Quick note*: I don't bid. Those three little words mean I only work on accounts where I control the process (re-read Alternatives to Bidding and Choosing a Broker pg. 82). Once I've gained a commitment and have entered the marketplace on behalf of a client I will spreadsheet the carriers with respects to terms, conditions and pricing. As a practice, I always include a column that shows my fee and or the percentage of commission that I will earn if they choose to bind with a specific carrier. On more than one occasion, the prospect will inquire what the commission percentage line is all about. I have to explain that insurance carriers will pay a commission based on a percentage of the premium. However, in an effort to be completely transparent with them, I didn't want them to think I was offering one carrier over another simply by which company put the most money in my pocket. I typically volunteer to share how much money I will be making when they bind the coverage. It's funny, the surprise expressions you will receive when candor and honesty is the rule of thumb. Along with consistency and reliability, transparency helps build credibility and trust. I know what you're thinking, "But, what business is it of theirs how much money I'm making?" Remember this. Transactions are smaller in nature and most people don't care how much profit goes into the pocket from a small sale. Relationship sales are larger in number (everyone's definitions of a large premium are different) and transparency equals trust.

"Always tell the truth, that way you don't have to remember what you said."
Samuel Clemens *aka* Mark Twain

Chapter 18
Six Additional Skills of the Sales Professional

With the acronym PALACES we discussed the mindset sales people need for success. With the PARC System we learned the potential "pains" that prospects can have and the qualifying questions pertaining to those concerns. There are four additional skills that the pros learn to master. There are entire books written on each of these skill sets discussed in this section. The goal here is to shine enough light on the subject to see the big picture of their importance in your sales success.

1.   Preparation

NFL Hall of Fame quarterback, Roger Staubach, says, "In business or in football, it takes a lot of unspectacular preparation to produce spectacular results." It's no different in sales. The better you prepare yourself, the better chances you have of winning. Pressure comes only when you are called upon to perform a task for which you have not prepared and preparing takes discipline. When it comes to discipline and routine, generally, sales people live and die by it. Routine instills discipline in your life and a reliable series of bench marks and activities you can follow over time to deliver predictable results. But, beware of falling into the trap of running every meeting the same way, losing sight of the fact that you're dealing with individuals.

On the old Tonight Show with Johnny Carson he would regularly interview famous comedians. These seasoned professionals knew their material inside and out. Johnny would ask a seemingly innocent and innocuous question and the funniest stories, lines and quotes would come from the comic. Great comedians have rehearsed their act over and over again and can weave their material into a conversation through proper preparation. Similarly, great sales people have rehearsed their questions and sales meeting agenda so well, that it seems natural to any first time prospect.

Regrettably, many of us don't prepare for first meetings the way we should. By preparation, I mean both in dress and in what they are expecting from the meeting (aim). Every salesman should know a few things about first meetings so that they can prepare adequately.

- Who is the meeting with (hopefully the decision maker)
- How long is the meeting supposed to last for
- What is the topic of conversation / agenda
- What are next steps moving forward (objective)

2. Prospecting Skills

Truth be told, most sales people don't like to plan. The classic argument is that it takes away from selling time in the field. I have uttered these very words, "I could sell more if I didn't waste time inputting pipeline data and filling out reports for management." For those that hate filling out reports, sorry, it's a necessary evil for tracking your progress and driving opportunities. Think of it as the "Aim," or goal of your business future. The most important thing to remember about pipelines is... you must be honest. Don't fill pipelines with accounts just to satisfy management. Be realistic (refer back to smart goals) and complete your pipeline with opportunities that are real. It's better to have 25 realistic opportunities than 50 fantasies. We've all heard, *"Most people don't plan to fail, they fail to plan."* Zig Ziglar.

- Do you plan for vacations?
- Do you plan for retirement?
- How many games would a team win if the coach didn't have a game plan?
- What would you think of a CEO who didn't have a plan?
- Would you invest in a new company if it didn't have a business plan?

George Santaya popularized the quote, *"Those who do not learn from history are doomed to repeat it."* Don't make the same mistakes over and over again. We plan other areas of our lives, it only makes sense to plan our sales careers. That's what pipelines help us do. Prospecting in today's environment has never been easier. The amount of information available today on key companies and their personnel is unparallel (thanks to big brother, I mean, the internet). You must know the essentials of the prospects company in order to *confirm* what you already know. Business owners appreciate it when they know you care enough to be prepared. One of the most ignorant statements any business owner will ever hear from a salesman is, *"Tell me about your company."* Imagine yourself as the CEO of your own territory. Take ownership, do your homework and differentiate yourself from the slackers. Depending on your "sweet spot," build your prospecting plan with a good mix of business. The most precious commodity for sales people is time. We've heard, *"The smaller and mid-size fish fill up the bucket faster than waiting for the big one."* Don't ignore the need to develop middle market and large accounts. Whatever size accounts you prospect, will most likely yield those types of accounts. If you concentrate on hunting middle-sized game, you will bag middle-sized game. (refer back to page 15 on account size)

The management mantra has always been, "It takes so many <u>no</u> responses to get to one <u>yes</u>." In the old days, we all knew this to be true. And in a sense, this is still true today, with one big caveat. Times have changed and too many of us have not changed with the times. What is the best and most efficient way to prospect the marketplace? Let's consider the multiple ways to prospect for new business. They could include (in no particular order):

➢ Mass Mailings
➢ Trade shows
➢ Cold Calling
➢ Networking
➢ Become the leader in your field so that people will seek you out
➢ Developing referral sources &
➢ Marrying the prospects daughter

Obviously, the best method of prospecting is when you don't have to do it at all. People naturally will seek you out when you're the leader in your field. Unfortunately, this takes a reputation, which takes time to build and time is not the friend of the quota. That leaves all the other forms (let's rule out marrying the prospects daughter). Sure, you can send crafty letters and other stuff to the decision makers (just like your competitors). My friend once tried prospecting Federal Express as a client and sent a UPS to the CFO. Yes, he was creative, got noticed and responded to, but didn't win the account. That kind of courage and boldness is the type of risk that every sales manager loves. Sending letters to the President/CEO then diligently following up does work and should be a part of your overall marketing campaign. However, there is an alternative. The method that changed the way I sold involved, developing relationships with key referral sources via networking. The Law of Reciprocity is similar to Newton's Law of Motion. Newton basically said for every action there is an equal and opposite reaction. The Law of Reciprocity essentially states, you reap what you sow. Helping other people get what they want first (without expecting anything in return) will come back to you with a blessing. Dialing for dollars, getting past gatekeepers and using methods to bypass screening is harder today than ever. The challenge is compounded if you're working in the same territory with a new employer under constraints of a non-compete. I found myself in this very position. Changing tactics, I asked myself,

- Who are the people with all the money?
- Who are the people with access to financials?
- Who puts deals together for businesses?

The answer: Banks, CPA's and Attorneys! Most likely, you've heard about the six degrees of separation for most people? Utilize your relationships to gain access to professionals in banks, accounting firms and law practices. When you meet with them, your agenda should be to find out how you can help their business grow. Then go find the type of client they are looking for and drive the referral. You must be diligent and have a willingness to help others get what they want. That's the very definition of altruism. Your return on investment (ROI) will reap huge dividends when you help others become successful.

One of my friends had left the insurance industry and just started working for a new payroll solutions company as an area manager. He introduced me to his first new hire and asked me if we might create some synergy by cross referring. They had a great solution that was extremely competitive and the competence level of the team was extremely high. We sat down and I started to call some friends and clients about potential opportunities. Another one of my friends has a company with about 400 employees and I asked them about their payroll. As it happened, they had just finished their due diligence with their payroll processing vendors and were going to make a change in the next 90 days. I asked them if they wouldn't mind looking at one more vendor. They agreed and I made the introduction. Long story short, my friend won their business, increased their proficiency, saved them more money and added time and attendance upgrades which decreased their overall costs. It was a win win scenario that I helped facilitate for two deserving business partners. Not only was it a win for both of them, but it also *decreased* my reputation as a vendor and *increased* my stature as a trusted advisor.

Obviously, building a rapport and relationship with referral sources takes some time. Investing in those relationships will be your greatest ROI. You will build friendships, your business, confidence and a reputation. In the end, your results will ultimately speak for themselves. One last universal truth. You will find that management tends to overlook reports when you become the consistent driving leader of revenue for corporate new business sales. Sales leaders get more slack.

"The only way on earth to influence other people is to talk about what they want and show them how to get it."
Dale Carnegie

3. Follow Up skills

Everyone knows the importance of follow up skills. Thankfully, with the age of the personal computer (PC) following up has never been easier. We no longer need shoe box file drawers of index cards with prospects expiration dates (X-Dates = expiration dates of the prospects policies) and business cards. There are dozens of options for contact and lead management programs that make reminders easy. The hard part is having the discipline to carve out uninterrupted time to actually do the follow up.

Let's suppose you're following up with next steps, what's the conversation going to sound like? Here's how it sounds for me. There is a common phrase that says, "There is a fine line between persistence and being a pain in the neck." I've used that line more than a few times, upon my follow up conversations with prospects. I wanted to let the prospect know I had not given up following through with my commitment to follow up with them. If I did not get a hold of my contact (decision maker) by the third time, I would leave a message that sounded something like this.

Mrs. ____, this is Paul Donovan with ____. I'm following up on our conversation we had last ____ where you asked me to call you about (PARC Method concerns identified). I know there's a fine line between persistency and being a pain in the neck and I never want to cross that line. Would you please call me back at (phone #) and let me know what my next steps are so we can avoid a restraining order, please and thank you."

A simple message, a touch of humor and being sincere typically got me a high return call percentage (or a restraining order). Save yourself problems when leaving a call back number. Remembers to annunciate clearly and with a slower cadence when leaving the return phone number. Nobody likes to listen to a long message over and over again because the phone number was garbled or spoken too quickly.

A disturbing trend that I see occurring more often in business is the move towards non-verbal communication. Can great relationships take place via twitter or texting? Answer: Yes, but it's Extremely Difficult! While it's true that a closed mouth gathers no foot, it's equally true that personalized communication speaks loudest and most effectively. Use the prospects name, wear a smile and be sincere. You'll be amazed how it comes through over the phone, Skyped or better yet, in person.

"Prospects are like phones. They want to know they can trust you through your actions but if you press the wrong button you'll get disconnected."
Paul Donovan

4. Post Analysis Skills Part One

No doubt, you've heard the saying attributed to everyone from Ben Franklin to Einstein, that the definition of insanity is doing the same thing over and over again and expecting different results. While I'm a huge proponent of learning from my mistakes, if I'm honest, I'd rather learn from the mistakes of others than have to go through the experience myself. Ah, the plight of the sales professional. At the end of every sales calls, whether successful or not, you must evaluate what you did right and what you could improve upon. The constant strain towards improvement is in the honest evaluation process. Unfortunately, I am not as objective when I critique myself.

- Did I ask the right questions?
- Did I listen and qualify statements?
- What commitments were made with the prospect?

To truly improve, try these exercises (you are going to think this is nuts.). Remember, there is no such thing as constructive criticism it's all unabashed criticism and you will need some thick skin.

1. Take another team member or manager to your next appointment. Use this time to have a third party honestly critique your skills and overall presentation. It's sobering and extremely helpful if you want to maximize your effectiveness. If you want to grow, you need them to be blunt and truthful without taking offense.

2. Once you qualify a prospect, you must set the expectations that a post debrief will be made irrespective if you win or lose the business. Let the prospect know that you will not try to influence their decision if you don't win the business. Ask permission from them to be candid with their feedback.

3. Lastly, hire a third party professional to conduct the interview. The critique will be the most objective you will get.

Post analysis exercises will teach you to focus your efforts on the buyer's reasons why they did or did not purchase from you. Knowing this information will shorten your learning cycle to determine what works and what doesn't. If you want to replicate success, post analysis is a sure fire way to improve results.

"This is one race of people for whom psychoanalysis is of no use whatsoever"
(Sigmund Freud - about the Irish).

5. Your Personal Debrief Part Two

If you were to ask the decision maker of the last sale you made, "Why did you purchase from me?" Could you definitively answer that question? What if they did not purchase from you, do you know the REAL reason why not? One of the reasons it can take so long to figure out how to duplicate sales success is because we neglect to find out WHY the decision maker ultimately made their choice. Whether you won the sale or lost the sale, you should absolutely make the commitment to find out why the decision was made. The perfect way to do that is with the debrief meeting. It will exponentially increase your learning curve and your win percentage.

The first step is setting the expectations with the prospect up-front.. At the end of your first meeting (after you have decided on next steps) you must prepare the prospect for a post interview, irrespective of you winning or losing the deal. Preparing the prospect in a non-threatening and permissive manner is critical. The conversation can go something like this.

Mrs. Prospect, thank you for your time today, I am looking forward to our next steps. Before I go, and with your permission, I would like to ask for your help with one more thing. At the end of the process, whether you decide to partner with us or not, I typically perform a post-interview. The interview takes just a few moments of your time. Instead of having to guess at what needs improvement I need to make, I use it to evaluate my skills as a consultative sales person. I'm my own biggest critic and open to any constructive feedback. Can I ask you to commit a few moments after all is said and done. Is that fair?

This non-threatening position will allow you to gain insight into what really happened during the decision making process. It will pay huge dividends in reinforcing good habits and changing areas you need to improve in.

A post interview should include some of these basic questions.

- In your opinion, what were the deciding factors in us (earning or not earning) your business?
- Did our competitors offer anything that we didn't? If so what?
- When it came down to us understanding your main concerns/issues, how do you think we did?
- What areas do you think I can most improve in?

If you don't earn the business now, don't forget to ask.... Would you be willing for us to keep in contact with you for a future opportunity? And most important of all when you win, don't forget to say thank you for allowing us the opportunity to earn your business. Typically a hand written note (yes hand written) is the extra touch in extra-ordinary service.

"All of us are born for a reason, but all of us don't discover why. Success in life has nothing to do with what you gain in life or accomplish for yourself. It's what you do for others."
Danny Thomas

6. Consulting and Brokering

Consultative sales involves:

- ✓ High ethical practices
- ✓ Attribute development areas
- ✓ Qualification questioning techniques
- ✓ Value added solution processes

The job of the broker is to pinpoint the concerns of the client, provide appropriate advice towards coverage options and then procure the best available program for the client. Most full line independent brokers can place all of your insurance needs. Having access to many of the top rated insurance carriers ensures a client that the best terms, conditions and rates are made readily available.

Occasionally, there are reasons when it makes more sense to become a paid consultant rather than to become the client's broker. The reasons could include; location, size and complexity or specialization of an account. For instance, I had a prospect that really wanted us to be their broker. However, they had a commercial aircraft that they needed to insure and our marketing capabilities were limited. The trust level was established and the client asked us to negotiate the contract for them acting as their risk manager. Knowing we could not be paid for the account, we charged a fee for the service. By volunteering services for a fee as a "temporary risk manager," you can still get paid for your efforts. Remember, never allow yourself to be in danger of becoming an unpaid consultant. Fees for service through a consultation agreement can quickly add revenue for your efforts. It is another way to create a win, win, win scenario. Many companies have a designated person that is typically wearing several "hats," and insurance is a small component of what they actually do. Having extensive experience and relationships with carriers (as well as with many of the top specialty brokerages) consultants are prepared to manage the process for and with a client. Consultants help alleviate the stress and shorten the learning curve by resolving all negotiations with brokers, underwriters, and loss control personnel. They can design service plans, help develop RFP specifications, analyze strategies, negotiate contract terms, conditions and fee structures to ensure all the appropriate resources/services are held accountable. Whether you split commissions; charge a flat fee for services or charge a percentage of savings, the client must receive quantifiable value and you must be paid for your efforts.

In some instances, I will bring in additional consultants on behalf of my client. This is not unusual when dealing with larger risks and specialty coverage. Specialty coverage could come in the form of a Captive Arrangement, International Risks, or an area that requires a specific license (ex: Crop Insurance). In some instance, brokers will negotiate a small percentage split of the commission with the broker that places the business, as an alternative to charging a fee.

It is critical to develop relationships with other consultants that you trust. Your reputation and relationship will be on the line, so do your due diligence. Remember, being transparent with the client regarding fees and commissions is pivotal to building a solid relationship of trust.

"If you're not part of the solution, there's good money to be made in prolonging the problem."

Larry Kersten about consultants

Chapter 19

Wrapping it all up

I have had the distinction of giving some rather poor advice as a young man. Back in the 1980's my wife and I were friends (still are) with another young married couple and they came to us with an opportunity they were thinking about entering into. They had visited a franchise exposition and picked up a brochure from a fledgling European styled west coast coffee company. They asked what I thought about the company. Remember, this is prior to the internet and research was a lot harder to perform. I looked at the pricing and quickly determined that in N.Y. there was a diner located on almost every corner. A cup of coffee costs fifty cents and I couldn't see why anyone would want to spend more than a dollar on a cup of coffee, especially from a start-up company named, "Starbucks." They agreed and decided to enter into other opportunities that they eventually became very successful in. The beauty of hindsight, and the experience of thirty seasons behind me in business, makes me hesitant to hand out rash advice that I'm not confident in. Thankfully, I'm confident that building your career on PALACES, and practicing the PARC method of qualifying can significantly increase your sales success.

Like most professions, a sales career is a constant process of becoming better each and every day. The battle goes to the persistent and the courageous. Growing up in a tough neighborhood, I found similarities between sales people and fighters. Great fighters possess the three essential components of strength, speed, and brains. Great fighters are strong, they need powerful muscles to be able to deliver a blow and take a blow. Likewise, great sales people are strong in their ability to develop relationships and new business opportunities. They also rely on their corner men/strong competent team members for support within their organization. Great fighters also have speed, and speed can overcome power every time. When you combine power and speed it is formidable both defensively and offensively. Sales teams that deliver quickly, consistently and efficiently typically have high retention levels, consistent referrals and a solid loyal customer base. The best fighters are smart. They have the knowledge from experience that being smarter than your opponent (educating yourself) always beats speed and power. That's why smart sales people are tenacious about developing winning strategies to grow and retain customers (adding value). Solutions can come from a host of areas, but the smartest strategy of all is creating a relationship with your client that the competition can't unseat. Like great fighters, great sales professionals like to win. Habitually helping your client's business thrive (giving them a win) will prove to be the ultimate partnership strategy of all. In the end this will build your credibility and trustworthiness.

I think back to the Old Testament book of Ecclesiastes and the writings of wise King Solomon. He said that there's nothing new under the sun, it's all been said and done before. Our technology has improved but our essential nature remains the same. Our search for answers and our quest for significance and success remain constant. The journey can be long and it is definitely filled with peaks and valleys. Once you've obtained a peak, expect a valley or two before the next view. The drive is always upward and onward, sometimes measured in inches rather than steps. What do I mean by that you ask?

In Rick Warren's bestselling book, <u>The Purpose Driven Life</u>, he has a chapter on *Seeing Life from God's View*. He asks, "How do you see your life?" Some say life is a circus, a minefield, a roller coaster, a puzzle, a symphony, a journey, a dance, and even a carousel (sometimes you're up, sometimes your down, and sometimes you just go round and round). Personally, I picture my life as a mountain climber. Life is a series of mountains in my range of life. I'm constantly climbing and conquering each new mountain, stopping every now and then to enjoy the view, resting, traveling through the valleys, then climbing again. That's the life of growth that we should all aspire towards. Trusting in the provision of God, to always do the right thing and knowing that I am only a steward. It's a temporary assignment so I manage the best I can, with His guidance, learned from the principles in His word.

"The mountains will bring prosperity to the people, the hills the fruit of righteousness."
Psalm 72:3

The Mountain

Dig deep for a few diamonds and a little bit of gold
The bounty will sustain you and provide when you are old

Caves hewn out of solid rock that nature did intend
Refuge for my protection, divinely He did send

The summer heat subsides in dark shadows it provides
Cleft for me to stand, filled with purpose for our lives

Winter snows they come and go majestic and sublime
Season's cycle bringing change with passages of time

Foundations anchored by His hand to comprehend I dare
It's only by His grace and love that saves me from despair

The eyes of those who have been closed see nothing in the plan
They're grounded in the winds of lies, from mountains made of sand

The mountain shades the harvest every season, all year long
If only I will stand close by, in weakness I'm made strong

Paul Donovan

Earl Nightingale said, "We are at our very best, and we are happiest, when we are fully engaged in work we enjoy on the journey toward the goal we've established for ourselves. It gives meaning to our time off and comfort to our sleep. It makes everything else in life so wonderful, so worthwhile." A career is more than being the best, meeting goals and making money, it's about fulfillment. Finding joy in the journey is the best part. Sometimes we make the process more complicated than we need to. We will never make a journey of a thousand miles by fretting about how long it takes or how hard it will be. We make the journey by taking each day step by step and then repeating it again and again until we reach our destination.

- Have you determined to have the right attitude in approaching your goals?

My sales career has been a journey of study, application and refinement. It has been filled with many great experiences and it continues to grow even today. It would not have been possible without serious investment, investment in myself and from others that poured their wisdom into my life. Your success will depend a lot on preparation and determination of your will to accomplish your goals. You must make a commitment to grow, educate, laugh and develop an attitude of excellence.

Parting comment:

Please remember, when you do experience success, do not forget to honor and thank those that helped you. In the chapter about Passion (pg. 22) we touched on Vince Lombardi's passion. His passion was about winning with a team. He also said, "Teamwork is what the Green Bay Packers were all about. They didn't do it for individual glory. They did it because they loved one another." Great teams accomplish great things. Teamwork builds trust and trust builds speed and efficiency. Honor your team and you will be honored. No sales person can go it alone and sustain success.

Be brave, be confident, resilient and humble. And, as Reba McIntyre said, "To succeed you need three things: A wishbone, a backbone and a funny bone."

Did you learn something? Anything? I hope you are encouraged and excited about the next traverse. In your journey may you keep climbing and never give up.

Please feel free to contact me, to encourage me with your success stories.

APPENDIX

The following appendix includes a generic sample questionnaire, a sample agency service agreement and a sample nondisclosure agreement. You should customize your agreements to fit your personal style, agency profile and income thresholds. Some of these services may or may not apply to your organization. These are samples only. For additional information on services, please refer to your corporate service team. For additional ideas please refer to IRMI, Inc. or your local Independent Agent Association.

SAMPLE QUESTIONAIRE

Date:
Client Name: Time Limit

NOT - <u>Naturally</u> you'll have some questions about Donovan Insurance Solutions, background, services, and examples of results experienced by our clients. <u>Obviously</u> I want to confirm what I already know about your company, culture, vision, and objectives. <u>Typically</u> at the end of our conversation we can discuss potential next steps, is that fair.

We understand the importance of most businesses insurance programs.   It's usually in the top 3 manageable expenses after payroll and taxes, but before we talk about insurance, I'd like to know.....

   a)   How did you come to the position you're in? Or

   b)   What was your greatest challenge last year? Or

   c)   How did your company handle the _____ I read about?

If you could describe the perfect vendor relationship, what would that look like and how would that impact your organization?

Like any good doctor or attorney, as an insurance professional I would never present solutions to a problem without first understanding what the problem is. Generally when I speak with businesses about their insurance program concerns they describe similar problems in what we call the PARC Method. It stands for .... I'd like to touch on any of those areas that you're trying to fix, accomplish or avoid, where would you like to start

Priorities

Premiums
Accountability   (Please see the PARC Chapter for your favorite questions)
Renewals
Resources
Relationships
Clams

Coverage
Communication

Besides yourself or in addition to yourself, how's the decision made? Then what?
Are there any other factors I should know about?
Does it make sense for us to get involved or can you see any reason not to
proceed? *Let's talk about next steps.*

<u>Notes</u>

AGENCY SERVICE AGREEMENT SAMPLE

We feel it is important for our clients to have an understanding of the services that will be provided by Donovan Insurance Solutions (DIS). The quotation on the insurance account is only the beginning. DIS will perform the following services for your company.

CURRENT POLICIES

1. **Policy Review** – Once the order has been received on a new account it is very important that coverage be carefully checked to make sure you are delivered what has been proposed. In addition to checking coverage, the policy rating is confirmed to make sure no errors were made.
2. **Coverage Checklist** – DIS prepares and provides you with a checklist of insurance exposures and available coverage. If coverage has been proposed and not taken, we will ask you to initial and refuse so that there will be no confusion should an uninsured loss occur.
3. **Insurance Summary and Cost Comparison** – DIS will prepare a summary of all of your insurance policies written, with a brief description of coverage and premium that should be useful to obtain a quick review of your insurance program. Please understand, however, that this is only a brief summary and does not reflect all of the provisions of the policies.
4. **Claim Forms and Claim Kit** – DIS has prepared a claim handling procedures kit that will explain the proper way to file a claim. Our office will work with you to make sure claims are handled properly and monitored on a timely basis. Our staff will assist you in settling claims and will keep you regularly updated as to claim status and resolution.

RENEWALS

1. **Renewal Meeting** – DIS will conduct a renewal meeting and a survey to determine your exposures for the coming year approximately 120 days prior to renewal. During this review we will discuss and request the following items from you.
a. Updated vehicle schedule
b. Updated equipment schedule
c. Payroll classifications for Workers Compensation
d. Estimate of Gross Annual Receipts for the upcoming year
e. List of current certificate holders
f. Property values for building and contents currently insured
g. List of named insured's
h. List of additional insured's
i. Uninsured motorist review
j. Request for driver information

2. **Annual Stewardship Report** – Within __ weeks after our renewal meeting, Donovan Insurance Solutions will prepare an annual report on such items as the following:
a. Summary of agency service activities during the past year
b. Brief review of major outstanding claims
c. Forecast of Workers Compensation and liability losses
d. Our views about the current marketplace and how it might affect your company
e. Summary of premium and loss experience
f. Goals and objectives for the coming year

3. **Classifications** – DIS recommends a comprehensive review of all policy classifications for Workers Compensation, automobile and general liability. The vehicle list will be carefully reviewed to make sure weights, usage, and garaging locations are correct. Of course, we will need your cooperation in performing this service.
4. **Certificates** – DIS recommends that certificate holders be provided new certificates __ days prior to your renewal with copies to the insured. If the renewal process is prompt, this can be easily accomplished. You will be supplied with completed certificates that can be executed from your office when needed. There is typically a __ hour turn-around-time on new requests
5. **Renewal Policies** – DIS endeavors to have renewal policies to our insured's prior to renewal. If this cannot be done for some reason, detailed binders will be prepared as confirmation of coverage.
6. **Summary Checklist** – DIS feels your renewal is more important than producing new business. We value our relationship together and try to never take our present clients for granted.

DAILY ACCOUNT SERVICES

Each agent has an account service team that works with them on the account. This account manager handles the day-to-day activity on your behalf. We recommend that your account administrator visit your facilities and meet with your personnel so that you can develop a good working relationship. Some of the areas in which we will provide service throughout the year are listed below.

1. **Audit** – The insurance audit is a very important function and should be coordinated by DIS so that a smooth and timely audit can be made. Periodically we will also recommend multiple audits throughout the year so that you can establish whether or not you are on target to meet your premium levels. We will try to notify you within ___ days after your renewal as to the timing of the audit. We'll discuss which records you should maintain so that you will not be overcharged in any area. Frequently, insured's are overcharged because of misclassification or the inappropriate application of a rating rule. Sometimes the exponential

growth or market shrinkage in your industry will contribute to premium adjustments. Our constant monitoring and communication should reduce the possibility of this happening to you. We will routinely review the audit for accuracy.

2. **Experience Rating** - DIS monitors your experience modification to ensure that no mistakes were made in the bureau calculation. We confirm claims audits to make certain that old reserves that have had no activity are not being carried in your experience modification. In some instances the application of analytic services can develop your claims data on your automobile and general liability insurance to impact savings. We will keep a record of your premium, broken down to base limits for bodily injury and property damage, along with loss information.

3. **Endorsements** – We will review all endorsements to make sure we have complied with your request. All endorsements and premium charges are checked for accuracy.

4. **Quarterly Loss Reports** – DIS will be provided a list of all claims for the major lines of coverage, on a quarterly basis.

5. **Quarterly Claims Meeting** – DIS will establish quarterly claims meetings with representatives of your company. The purpose will be to review open claims and discuss their closing and final resolution.

6. **Retrospective Premium Calculations** – Final retrospective premium calculations will be provided no later than __ months after expiration of the applicable policy period. We will review these adjustments before sending them to you to reduce the possibility of mistakes.

7. **Location Visits** – Our staff, in conjunction with the insurance company, will visit plants on an as needed basis to evaluate unique loss exposures associated with your operations.

8. **Communications** – DIS will communicate with you frequently to discuss any particular issues, concerns, or initiatives not previously addressed within the service agreement. We will be available on request to provide research assistance and consultation on risk management issues that may be of concern to you.

9. **Contract Documents** – DIS will review business contracts you furnish us from a risk management and insurance perspective and provide you with our analysis. We suggest that whenever possible, you let us see contracts before executing them in case an attempt to negotiate changes should be made. We make contract reviews only with the understanding that we are not attorneys and cannot give you a legal opinion. All contracts should be carefully reviewed by qualified legal counsel.

ACCEPTED BY:

_____   DATE _____

_____   DATE _____

SAMPLE NONDISCLOSURE & CONFIDENTIALITY AGREEMENT

It is understood and agreed to that the below identified discloser of confidential information may provide certain information that is and must be kept confidential. To ensure the protection of such information of both parties, and to preserve any confidentiality necessary it is agreed that:

1. The Confidential Information to be disclosed can be described as and includes: Policy information, business information relating to your insurance program(s), proprietary ideas, strategies, pricing, underwriting information, projections, marketing, and risk management / loss controls, cost containment measures and resource allocations regardless of whether such information is designated as "Confidential Information" at the time of its disclosure.

2. The Recipient shall limit disclosure of Confidential Information within its own organization to its directors, officers, partners, members, employees and/or independent contractors (collectively referred to as "affiliates") having a need to know. The Recipient and affiliates will not disclose the confidential information obtained from the discloser unless required to do so by law.

3. This Agreement imposes no obligation upon Recipient with respect to any Confidential Information (a) that was in Recipient's possession before receipt from Discloser; (b) is or becomes a matter of public knowledge through no fault of Recipient; (c) is rightfully received by Recipient from a third party not owing a duty of confidentiality to the Discloser; (d) is disclosed without a duty of confidentiality to a third party by, or with the authorization of, Discloser; or (e) is independently derived by Recipient.

4. This Agreement states the entire agreement between the parties concerning the disclosure of Confidential Information. Any addition or modification to this Agreement must be made in writing and signed by the parties.

5. If any of the provisions of this Agreement are found to be unenforceable, the remainder shall be enforced as fully as possible and the unenforceable provision(s) shall be deemed modified to the limited extent required to permit enforcement of the Agreement as a whole.

WHEREFORE, the parties acknowledge that they have read and understand this Agreement and voluntarily accept the duties and obligations set forth herein.

Recipient of Confidential Information: Name (Print or Type):

Signature: Date:

Discloser of Confidential Information: Name (Print or Type):

Signature: Date:

SAMPLE Consulting Agreement

This agreement is made this day _____ of 20___, by and between Donovan Insurance Solutions, whose address is 858 Briar Oak Ct. Tarpon Springs, FL 34689, hereinafter referred to as the "Consultant", and _____, whose principal place of business is located at _____, hereinafter referred to as "Company".

NOW THEREFORE, for and in consideration of the premises and the mutual covenants hereinafter entered into, the parties agree as follows:

1. <u>Terms of Agreement.</u> The engagement shall commence as of _____ and shall continue to and including _____. This Agreement can be extended by mutual consent of the parties hereto upon the same terms and conditions for a period of time as agreed upon by the parties.

2. <u>Duties.</u> Consultant shall provide the Company with his best advice, information, judgement and knowledge regarding insurance and risk management assistance including and not limited to insurance program design and development of services to Client.

3. <u>Time Requirements.</u> Consultant agrees to furnish Client with consulting services as required by Client and as mutually agreed upon in advance by the parties hereto. Client desires to retain the services of Consultant for the initial period of _____ (__) calendar months, and Consultant is willing to perform the services called for upon the terms and conditions set forth in this Agreement.

4. <u>Relationship.</u> Consultant is retained by Client solely for the purposes and to the extent set forth in this Agreement, and Consultant's relationship to Client shall during the terms of this Agreement be that of an independent contractor.

5. <u>Consultations.</u> Consultant shall be available to consult with the Board of Directors, the officers of the Company, and the heads of the administrative staff, at reasonable times, concerning matters pertaining to the organization

of the administrative staff, insurance policies of the Company, the relationship of the Company with its employees or with any organization representing its employees, and, in general, the important problems of concern in the business affairs of the Company. Consultant shall not represent the Company, its Board of Directors, its officers or any other members of the Company in any transactions or communications nor shall Consultant make claim to do so.

6. Liability. With regard to the services to be performed by the Consultant pursuant to the terms of this agreement, the Consultant shall not be liable to the Company, or to anyone who may claim any right due to any relationship with the Corporation, for any acts or omissions in the performance of services on the part of the Consultant or on the part of the agents or employees of the Consultant, except when said acts or omissions of the Consultant are due to willful misconduct or gross negligence. The Company shall hold the Consultant free and harmless from any obligations, costs, claims, judgments, attorneys' fees, and attachments arising from or growing out of the services rendered to the Company pursuant to the terms of this agreement or in any way connected with the rendering of services, except when the same shall arise due to the willful misconduct or gross negligence of the Consultant and the Consultant is adjudged to be guilty of willful misconduct or gross negligence by a court of competent jurisdiction.

7. Compensation & Retainer . The Client shall pay Consultant the sum of $_____ per hour or a flat fee of $_____ for services performed and rendered to the Company pursuant to the terms of the agreement. Client shall pay consultant the sum of $_____ for travel time when such travel is authorized by client. Travel time includes all time spent between departure from origination and arrival at destination, inbound and outbound, minus any time therein during billable services are performed. Consultant shall present an invoice to Client each month for services performed, travel time and expenses. Payment shall be due in full within 30 days of the date of invoice.

8. Confidentiality. Consultant shall treat as confidential and shall not disclose or use for the benefit of any person other than Client any and all information made available or disclosed to Consultant as a result of or related to the Business Consultant Agreement; provided, however, Consultant shall have no obligation hereunder as to any portion of such

information which is disclosed by Client to others without any restriction on use and disclosure.

9. Waiver, Alteration, or Cancellation. Any waiver, alteration, or modification of any of the provisions of this Agreement or cancellation or replacement of this Agreement shall not be valid unless in writing and signed by the parties. This agreement may be terminated by either party giving thirty (30) days' written notice to the other party at the addresses stated above or at an address chosen subsequent to the execution of this agreement and duly communicated to the party giving notice. Any attempt to assign or transfer any rights, duties, or obligations herein shall render such attempted assignment or transfer null and void.

10. <u>Governing Law& Arbitration.</u> This Agreement shall be construed in accordance with and governed by the laws of the State of Florida. Any controversy or claim arising out of or relating to this contract, or the breach thereof, shall be settled by arbitration in accordance of the rules of the American Arbitration Association, and judgment upon the award rendered by the arbitrator(s) shall be entered in any court having jurisdiction thereof. For that purpose, the parties hereto consent to the jurisdiction and venue of an appropriate court located in Pinellas County, State of Florida. In the event that litigation results from or arises out of this Agreement or the performance thereof, the parties agree to reimburse the prevailing party's reasonable attorney's fees, court costs, and all other expenses, whether or not taxable by the court as costs, in addition to any other relief to which the prevailing party may be entitled. In such event, no action shall be entertained by said court or any court of competent jurisdiction if filed more than one year subsequent to the date the cause(s) of action actually accrued regardless of whether damages were otherwise as of said time calculable.

IN WITNESS WHEREOF, the parties have hereunto executed this Agreement on the_____ day of_____ , 20____ .

_____ (Client)   _____ (Consultant)

Date _____   Date_____

Title: _____   Donovan Insurance Solutions

Paul Donovan - President

Acknowledgements

How I am thankful and grateful to my loving wife Jan is inexpressible. When we got married in 1986 she had no idea that I would rarely ever have a salary and that we would eat what I euphemistically could kill through commission sales. The faith that we both developed in the provision of God for our lives all these years has been unmistakable. Her consistent love, honesty, devoted support and encouragement for everything I have ever attempted is remarkable. Volumes could be written about her character, I am exceedingly blessed! I thank God for my two sons Kevin and Connor, who have always had a roof over their head, food in their stomachs and a grateful smile on their faces.

My father, David Donovan, started me down this career path, teaching me about risk/reward. He passed away on St. Patrick's Day 2010, an insurance professional like no other. Special thanks to Royal & Bena Rollins, Sonny & Nancy Lenoci, Dick & Marilyn Whitman, Jennifer Julius, and Sharon Seifert, my family that has been with me throughout. My great friend Dean "Mr. Generous" Tanella - teaching me the joy in pursuit of professionalism. To Mrs. Marty Giancola and Mrs. Ann Gianeskis for their constant encouragement. Every week for over a dozen years, Mark Gianeskis & Andy Giancola meeting for breakfast and accountability, wow. To Dr. J.P. Gills & Heather Gills I owe an infinite amount of gratitude for being one of the wisest couples I know, mentoring through their lifestyle of excellence. Two great business partners, Bill Kelsey & Terry Russell, men with character and integrity beyond measure and a constant support. Thanks to my friends Mike Casey for teaching me about listening skills and Joe Mello as Mr. Bold. To Mr. Romeo Francis - my first manager and a great salesman. Jim Marshall - a fantastic Sandler Sales teacher and entrepreneur. Bud Day thank you for your help. Pastor Herb Lang - encouraging and empowering everyone to be strong in their faith. To my friend Ginny Gause thank you for getting me out of my comfort zone and making me think.

A debt of thanks for additional great authors (please see pg. 39): Jack

Welch, William S. McIntyre IV, Jack P. Gibson, Neil Rackman, David Mattson, Jeffrey Gittomer, Michael Q. Pink, Robert A. Bregman (IRMI, Inc.) and Napoleon Hill. The diversity of experience, knowledge and wisdom that each of these people have contributed to me through their writings is available to all.

What an incredible journey of growth and discovery through trial, some error, and a multitude of success. Most important, is my thankfulness to my Lord and Savior Jesus Christ. My faith creates my core values and I aspire to let it drive every motive I have. With exceeding gratitude, faith and obedience I am following the call.

Connect with Me Online: Donovan.Solutions@gmail.com

www.DonovanInsuranceSolutions.com

Twitter: http://twitter.com/@PaulDonovan1

Facebook: http://facebook. http://www.Paul Donovan.com

About the Author

Paul Donovan began his career in 1986 working with a large national firm in the New York City metro area. In 1991 he transferred to FL working with an independent agency for ten years before making partner. He left that firm and spent another decade working for two of the top five national brokerage houses. He was responsible for developing middle market P&C and Workers Compensation accounts. In 2011 he started Donovan Insurance Solutions in Tarpon Springs, FL.

www.ingramcontent.com/pod-product-compliance
Lightning Source LLC
Chambersburg PA
CBHW051317170526
45166CB00002B/579